THE WALL OF FAME
NEW YORK CITY'S LEGENDARY MANNY'S MUSIC

THE WALL OF FAME

NEW YORK CITY'S LEGENDARY MANNY'S MUSIC

BY HENRY GOLDRICH AND HOLLY GOLDRICH SCHOENFELD

HAL•LEONARD®

Jacket design by Shane Konen
Book interior by Kevin Hein

Archival advertisements, courtesy of NAMM Resource Center

Published by Hal Leonard Corporation
7777 Bluemound Road
P.O. Box 13819
Milwaukee, WI 53213

Trade Book Division Editorial Offices
19 West 21st Street
Suite 201
New York, New York 10010

Library of Congress Control Number: 2006936122
ISBN 1-4234-0555-2

Printed in the United States of America
First Edition

Hal Leonard books are available at your local bookstore, or you may order through Music Dispatch at 1-800-637-2852 or www.musicdispatch.com.

Acknowledgments

This book is for the miracles in my life, Hannah Jade and Sammy Alden.

I would like to thank all the people who have supported me through this project: my brothers Ian and Judd; my nieces and nephews, family, and friends; my husband Douglas; and especially my parents, Henry and Judi.

Thank you to the following people for their assistance: editor Mike Edison and the entire team at Hal Leonard – John Cerullo, Belinda Yong, and Jenna Young. Thanks to Dan Del Fiorentino at NAMM for providing archive images, Chris Teenager for his help in pulling pictures from the wall, and all the artists who shared their Manny's experience for this book.

Marc, you are always with me.

Holly Goldrich Schoenfeld

A FEEDING FRENZY OF AMERICANA
Paul Simon Remembers Manny's

Henry sold me my first guitar, an electric Epiphone, sometime in the late '50s. I went there with my Dad, who was a bassist. I must have been fourteen. I was still playing rock'n'roll — I didn't switch to acoustic until after the '50s.

But I had met Henry years before, in the old Manny's store, when my Dad would go to buy rosin or strings for his bass. I remember going there as a little kid, and I have very fond memories of that place, memories I associate with my father, and this incredible time in New York. There was a big music scene before rock'n'roll. Down 52nd Street, there was Birdland and all those places, and my father worked at Roseland. We would come in to the city to watch my father work. It was very exciting. And Manny's was the big music store of the time.

The first guitars I bought were all from Manny's. I was in there a lot. The Guild guitars that I used on all the Simon and Garfunkel records either came from Guild directly or I got them from Manny's.

I don't remember exactly when I gave him the first photo, but I felt good about having it up there. It was a special kind of thing — he knew me since I was eight, and had watched me grow into a successful musician. And then it became his store, and I knew him through those changes, too.

When I was a teenager, I used to roam around that area with Artie Garfunkel, and Manny's was one of the hubs of the music scene. It was the first store to make the transition from my father's generation of musicians to kids like me, who wanted their first amps and guitars to play rock'n'roll. Manny's evolved with rock'n'roll, and Henry did that. He had an easy relationship with musicians, I think because he wasn't impressed. Coming out of New York at that time, being a store owner, you had to have a certain kind of toughness. He was a straight-ahead guy.

Before Simon and Garfunkel became a hit I was living in England, and I knew some of the guys, like Graham Nash from the Hollies, and some of the other musicians in the first wave of the British Invasion, and they were going to Manny's, too. The place in London that was the equivalent was Wardour Street. That's where there were music publishers and a few guitar stores with stuff in the window. But the stuff they had wasn't nearly the quality of American guitars, and they were very expensive. At Manny's they were able to get good equipment at good prices, and there was a feeding frenzy of Americana and quality instruments.

Henry has known me since before I made it. He knew my father, and I knew his father, so our memories really go back a long time. More than fifty years. I like Henry. I've liked Henry since I was a kid! And I like his family. They were good people in a very good time in my life. I have a well of affection for them.

Paul Simon
Calling from Arizona
July 2, 2006

Henry and Holly, Manny's Music, 2006

FOR THOSE ABOUT TO ROCK

This has been a labor of love. Henry Goldrich, my Dad, is my hero. I really am daddy's little girl!

I grew up in Manny's. I used to play hide and go seek in the stacks of Marshall amps. Manny's was my life. There was always someone special in Manny's. It was such a happening place. I remember when Mick Jagger and David Bowie came in together and the entire street just shut down. But Dad treated everyone the same, always with respect. You could be the kid next door just buying a pair of drum sticks with your allowance, or Ringo Starr, and you got the same treatment. Celebrities? You name 'em, Henry knew them all, and he always kept me by his side while he was schmoozing. I was so lucky to be there. What he really loved was to see kids go from nothing, to making it, and then making it to the wall.

My father is unconditional with his love, and I saw so much because of him. My brothers and I were so lucky to go to all the shows of all the bands and musicians that came in to the store — I remember he took us to see Sly and the Family Stone, I think I was only about four years old!

Dad is a great man with a great heart and a great legacy. Musicians always knew about Manny's, and they knew how special my dad is. Now everyone will know.

Henry is too humble to realize the impact he's made. He has touched so many so gracefully, and he is in awe of these people who are coming out to help us do this book, and saying such wonderful things.

Lately, Dad looks after my mom, Judi, and there is so much love there, it is just a fantastic affirmation of this man's heart. They love each other so much, and I love them both, too. I am so happy and so proud to be able to do this book with him.

This book is a gift to my grandfather, my parents, my family, and my friends, to all the musicians who ever came through Manny's and shared their dreams with us, for those in Heaven, and for those about to rock. We love you.

Holly Goldrich Schoenfeld

Manny Goldrich
April 15, 1905 – May 25, 1968

THE WALL OF FAME

NEW YORK CITY'S LEGENDARY MANNY'S MUSIC

The Beatles made the music business.

The first time we heard of the Beatles was when the guys from the big cruise ships, the Queen Mary or the Queen Elizabeth, the musicians who played on those boats, would come in when they were docked in New York.

And when they came in we had to practically close up the store up because they bought so much stuff to take back to England. It was so much cheaper here. They'd buy all sorts of accessories and instruments to sell in Europe.

"I loved the Beatles. They had tons of class."

They could quadruple their money by bringing these items back. Everybody wanted American guitars.

The British invasion started right around then, '61 or '62, and the first British group to come in was the Nashville Teens. They knew nothing about New York, but they did know of Manny's and they came there right after getting off the plane. These guys were amazed at New York City, and amazed at the music store. The stores in England didn't have anything like we had. They used to tell me about this group called the Beatles. I never heard of them, of course. I used to make fun of them, and call them the "Bootles."

They didn't know where to stay, so I got them rooms at the Bristol hotel, across from the store. After

Gibson J-160e

MANNYS
CIRCA 1965

they left, the influx started, and not a day went by without some superstar coming into Manny's.

Gerry and the Pacemakers were here. I became very friendly with Herman's Hermits. They practically lived here. They used to come to the store in their limousines, and they never understood how the girls knew they were going be at Manny's. (They had a good press agent.) When they got there, there would be a whole group

THE BYRDS   PERENCHIO/ARTISTS' REPRESENTATIVE

of screaming fans in front of the store.

They used to run into the store — and they always wore these wild little outfits, the English blue bonnet type of outfits. They were very cute. They'd run into the store, and up the stairs, and we'd block the way so nobody could get up there. They'd try out all of this stuff and spend several thousand dollars. And they did that a lot! They were an amazingly funny group, they had more playfulness in them than anyone. There was never a bad word out of their mouth. They were so happy with where they were. Probably because they were average musicians. Peter Noone, the singer, he's an actor. He never was a musician, he just happened to make it.

I liked the Yardbirds, too. Jimmy Page, Jeff Beck, and Eric Clapton. Of course later all of them played with different groups. When Clapton first got started, he used to buy a lot of guitars. He played both Fenders and Gibsons. But I think he liked Fenders best of all.

Years later, when he was on the downs, and needed money, he came in to my store, and I bought the amps he was using with Cream. He needed the money, and I paid him cash for them. He was very thankful, and still, when he comes to New York and "forgets" his guitars, he'll call us and we'll lend him a Stratocaster. And then he signs the guitar, which we sell — but we never made that much money on his things.

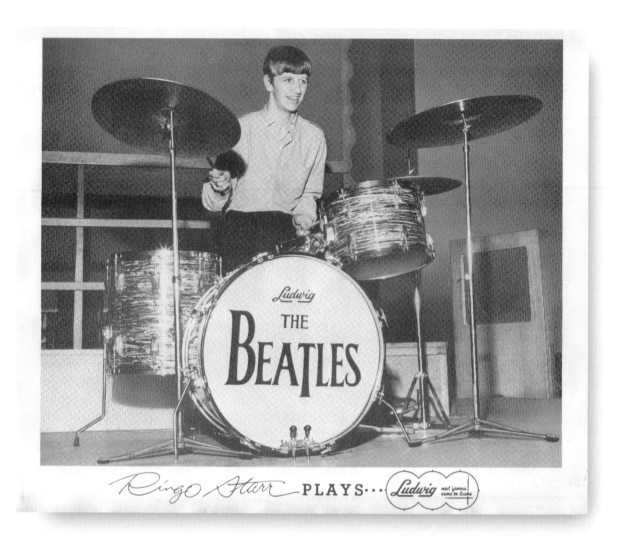

Ringo Starr PLAYS... Ludwig most famous name on drums

Like I said, the Beatles, really, made the music business. They took it from where it was, a small family business, and made it gigantic. The first time they came in, it was George Harrison and Ringo Starr, and they wandered in during the busiest time of the day. They were quite noticeable; they were wearing multicolored, beautiful clothing. I wanted to help them myself, but the store was jammed, but we pride ourselves on our musician customers. I told them that I had nobody to take care of them right away, but to feel fee to try out whatever they wanted. They were so great, they hung around for an hour or so, signed autographs,

VOX: sound of the longhairs

Like the Beatles   Like the Rolling Stones   Like the Dave Clark Five

And the Animals. Billy J. Kramer & The Dakotas.
Freddie & The Dreamers. Petula Clark.
The Searchers. All the top groups.
Let your hair down and go with the sound
of VOX. Send us the coupon. We'll send
you the address of your VOX dealer—plus
information on the complete VOX line.

The YOUNG RASCALS

and purchased several thousand dollars worth of accessories. They got most of their instruments for promotion, but they wanted to try effects and they sure did buy a lot of stuff. Ringo purchased every sort of drum gizmo there was. It took three trips to put all the stuff in the limo.

After that, the Beatles came in quite frequently, and when they did, all of them were perfect gentlemen, never asking to be served first. They would sit down quietly, they signed autographs. They were completely marvelous people. I loved the Beatles. They had tons of class.

When they played at Shea Stadium, Ringo had had a problem with his

THE ANIMALS

SUITE 306
200 W. 57th STREET
NEW YORK NY 10019

"How can a block of solid wood sound so good? How're you gonna sell something like that?"

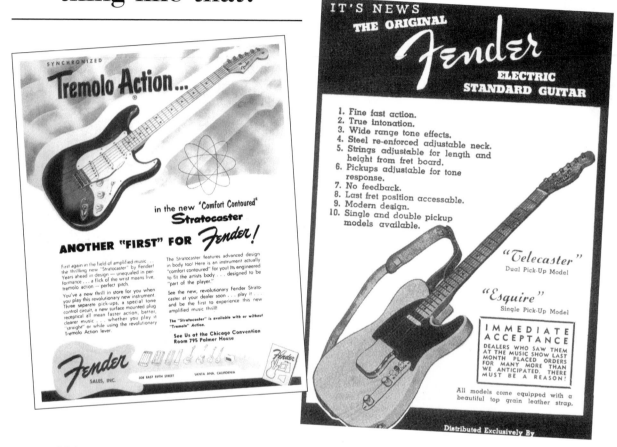

hi-hat — we got the emergency call at Manny's. My brother in law, Danny Burgauer, a drummer, understood the problem, so after picking out the smoothest unit we had, Danny drove it out to Shea. Ringo was so desperate for it that Danny had no trouble getting through the mob scene. But he didn't stay to see the show. And he was already backstage. Boy, he was sorry later on.

A few years later John Lennon found a Gibson J-200 flat top jumbo guitar that he really liked. He told me that he would put it on the cover

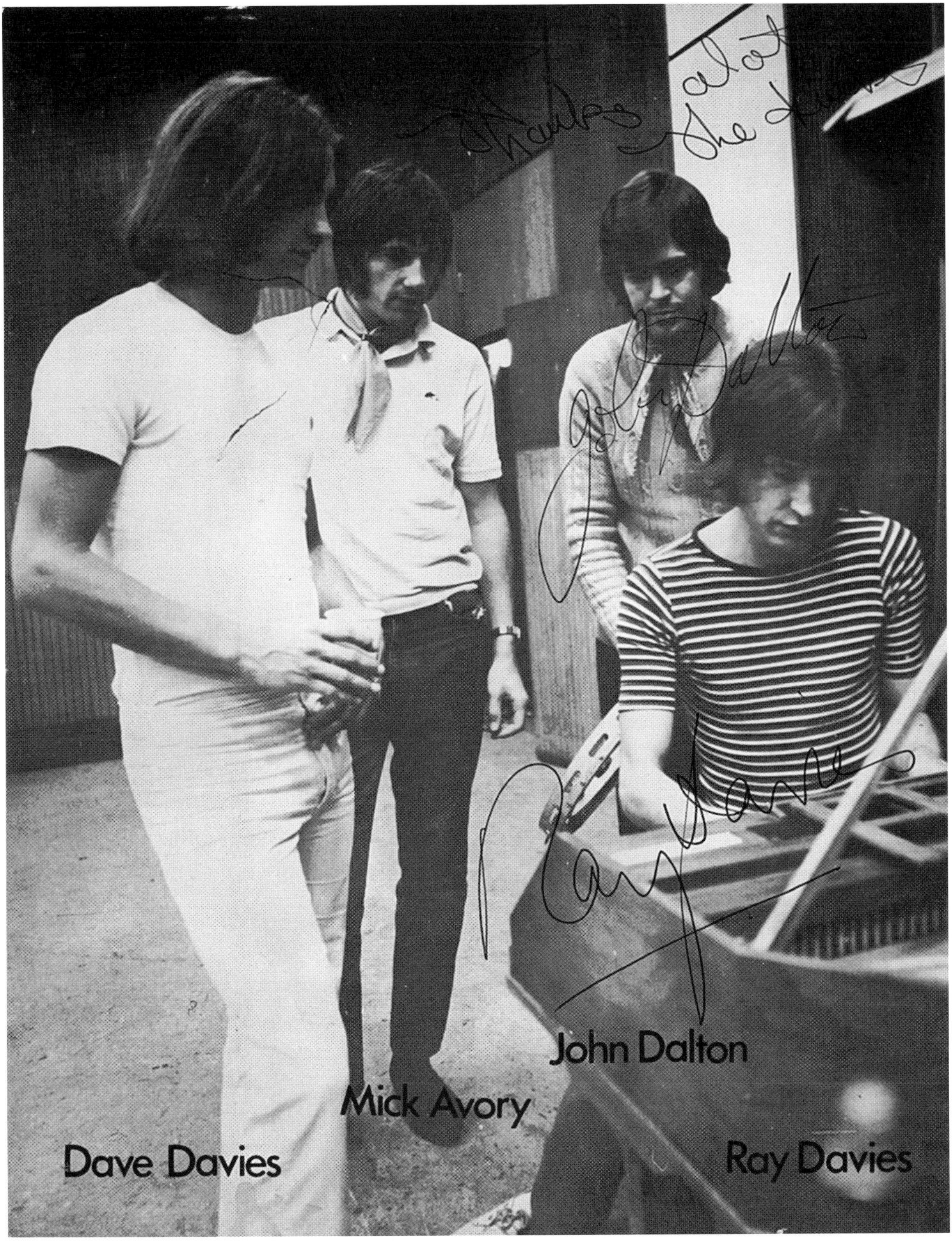

Mick Avory

John Dalton

Dave Davies

Ray Davies

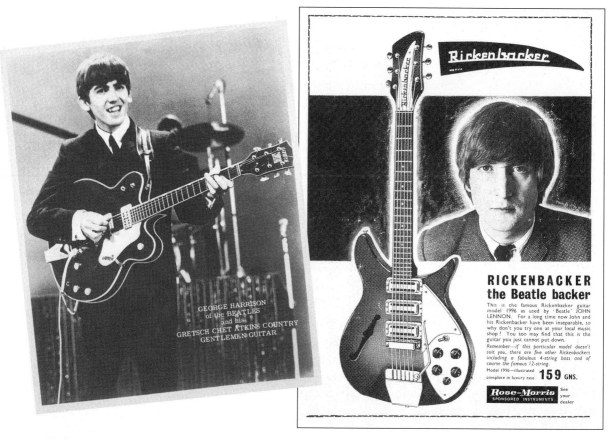

GEORGE HARRISON
of the BEATLES
and his
GRETSCH CHET ATKINS COUNTRY
GENTLEMEN GUITAR

Rickenbacker

RICKENBACKER
the Beatle backer

This is the famous Rickenbacker guitar model 1996 as used by 'Beatle' JOHN LENNON. For a long time now John and his Rickenbacker have been inseparable, so why don't you try one at your local music shop? You too may find that this is the guitar you just cannot put down.
Remember—if this particular model doesn't suit you, there are five other Rickenbackers including a fabulous 4-string bass and of course the famous 12-string.
Model 1996—illustrated complete in luxury case **159** GNS.

Rose-Morris See
SPONSORED INSTRUMENTS your
dealer

of their next album if Gibson would give it to him. I called Les Propp, who was president of the company, and asked him what he wanted to do. John was standing right next to me. At that time Gibson was giving nothing away, but he told me that Lennon could have the guitar for manufacturing cost, which was less than my cost. John said "no thank you," but still bought the guitar from me. But Gibson missed out at being on the cover of *Magical Mystery Tour*. What a loss for Gibson and for Manny's.

One day, Paul McCartney called to see if we had any clay ocarinas.

Paul's Hofner violin bass.

14

THE ROLLING STONES   CREATIVE MANAGEMENT: ANDREW LOOG OLDHAM
DIRECTION: ALLEN KLEIN

Suite 4326
Time & Life Bldg.
New York City
CI 5-7

"On Sundays, a truck would pull up in front of my store, with two or three hundred Fender guitars and amplifiers."

We had just gotten a shipment. An hour later this young lady came in, purchased one in every key, and gave my wife Judi a check. Judi wasn't going to take it, because Linda, Paul's wife, did not have proper ID, and Judi didn't know her. But we did take her check, and Paul called us up personally to thank us.

Several weeks before John was killed, Yoko and John came in to look for a piano. After going through the whole litany of pianos they decided

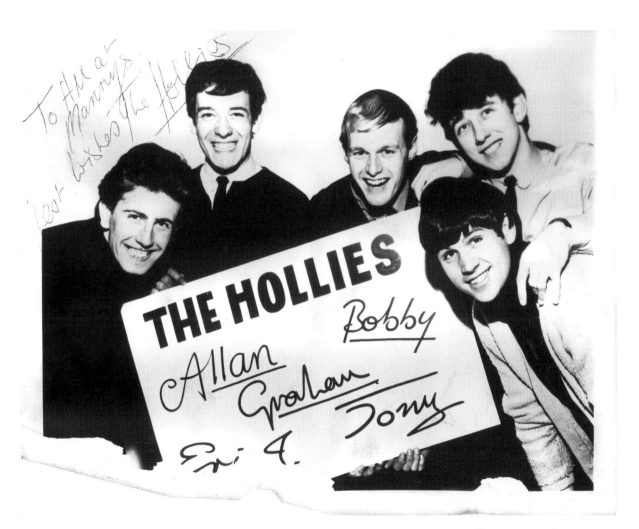

on a Yamaha C-70. A very large unit that we had to deliver to the
Dakota. The funny part of this story is that they were so incognito that
no one noticed who they were. The store was busy, but no one, and I
mean no one, went near them.

When the Beatles first came to New York, all the companies made our
store the focal point. So every company sent us in the equipment for
the Beatles. Ludwig drums c/o Ringo Starr. Hofner basses for Paul. John
Lennon had a Rickenbacker. I'm sure in the beginning he had a Fender,
too. George Harrison had a Gretsch, as well. They both had Gisbon
acoustics, the J-160e. They played everything.

Gibson
Les Paul model

It's a Sensation!

Designed by Les Paul—produced by Gibson—and enthusiastically approved by top guitarists everywhere. The Les Paul Model is a unique and exciting innovation in the fretted instrument field; you have to see and hear it to appreciate the wonderful features and unusual tone of this newest Gibson guitar. Write Dept. 101 for more information about it.

It wasn't just the Fenders and the Gibson electrics that were so popular; a lot of guys used what they called "dry guitars," the big acoustics. Dry. No electricity, nothing.

But when the Fender craze hit, and the Gibson craze hit, which was the early 1950s, everybody started buying them. And at that time, I was on the outs with Leo Fender. I don't remember why. I think it was because my uncle, who was in the store at the time, never thought a solid-body guitar would make it, and he teased Leo Fender about it. We said, "How

"Les is a genius. He did things with a guitar that no one else could."

can a solid block of wood sound good? How're you gonna sell something like that?" and then six months later we ate our words. There were other solid-bodies on the market, but nothing that had the sound, the rock sound that the Fender had.

One of the things that made Fender was the Stratocaster, with the whammy bar — their vibrato system, that was hugely popular. The Bigsby vibrato arm was before that, but when Fender came out with the Stratocaster, everyone wanted it. We never thought they were going to take off. The guy that sold for Leo Fender, a guy named Mike Cole, ended up making so much money that he bought a hundred-and-some-odd-foot yacht from selling those guitars.

So we tried to carry the Fender line — but Leo Fender would never give it to us. So we used to buy them from other stores. On Sundays, a truck would pull up in front of my store, with two or three hundred Fender guitars and amplifiers. We made some dealers the biggest Fender dealers in the country. No one else could have done it — you know, we bought from five or six different dealers, so we had everything in stock.

Rickenbacker

The World's Most Distinguished Name in Guitars, Amplifiers and Accessories

SPANISH GUITARS

The Gibson Les Paul also came out in the early '50s, and at first it wasn't as popular as the Fenders. The Fenders were lighter and had a greater variety of sounds. And Fender had different designs. The Gibson solid-body was just the Les Paul.

Les Paul was paid for every guitar sold with his name on it. It was an unbelievable amount of money.

Les is a genius. He did things with a guitar that no one else could do. He made effects that no one else could, and whatever he did, he had a touch of gold; he was really good. Strange, but good.

The Les Paul has a very cutting sound, but it was still a sweeter-sounding guitar than the Fenders. And all of the Gibson thin-line guitars, the semi-hollow body electrics, became exceedingly popular after a while. The 335, that was a great guitar. The Beatles liked the Epiphone Casino, which was made by Gibson.

A lot of companies came out and tried to make a guitar that was halfway in-between Fender and Gibson, but you can't. You can't copy either of them. There are a lot of successful companies, but they'll never have the prestige of Gibson or Fender.

THE JIMI HENDRIX EXPERIENCE

Jimi Hendrix was probably my best customer.

He came into the store for the first time before he was famous. He was playing with a guitarist, Curtis Knight. Curtis Knight had a little rock band here in New York City. Curtis had been a good customer of mine for many years, so when Jimi came in and wanted a guitar for $225 or $230, and he only had $100, so we gave him credit.

Jimi told me he'd be back in two or three weeks. Since my father used to let the musicians charge merchandise in the old days, I figured it was a good thing to keep it going. One month goes by, two months go by, three months. I forgot all about it.

One day this guy comes into the store and says, "I owe you money." I had no idea what he was talking about. "Well, I charged a guitar when I was with Curtis Knight, and I want to pay you." And he paid me. And from there on in, he never, to my knowledge, for the next year and half, bought a guitar in any other music store.

Jimi became very famous. He came into the store all the time, and he became a very good customer of mine. At first I didn't realize how famous he was. He would come into the store and buy two or three guitars, four guitars, two or three amplifiers, and every new sound device I had.

He used to come in during the day. It was a little much for him because he was a very shy person. He asked me to stay open after six o'clock, when we usually closed. He was such a good customer that I

LED ZEPPELIN

From left   right: Jimmy Page,   ohn

Bonha   obert Plant and J   aul Jones.

CREAM

said fine, no problem. He came in and he used to charge guitars, amps, like I said, every effect we had, and God knows how many strings. He would sign it to his accountant's office. One evening he came in, and my mother was at the cash register. He bought all this stuff, and charged it, and he gave my mother a ten-dollar tip. He said, "Mama, this is for staying open late." My mother, of course, took it, even though he knew who she was.

This went on for many years. We used to soup up his guitar for him. All his pickups were hot-wired so they were more powerful than normal. I was a pretty good guitar repairman, I knew how to fix Jimi's guitars to make him happy.

One day he came into the store, a real nasty, rainy day. Jimi bought like five guitars, eight amplifiers. It was an amazing amount of merchandise.

Jim Marshall

"Pete Townshend loved the tone, but wanted it louder."

Manny's Music store stocked and sold so much Marshall gear — they were my number one dealer.

The personal relationship between me and the musicians who visited my shop in Hanwell was vital to the development of the Marshall range, and indeed the stack. Pete Townshend and Ritchie Blackmore regularly visited and told me the kind of sound they wanted from their amps, and asked

me to make an amp for them. They would say that the Fender Bassman was somewhere near rock 'n' roll, but a bit too far away.

So, with Ken Bran and Dudley Craven, I made six prototypes, and the last one had the sound I heard in my head. This would be the sound of Marshall from now on, and has been ever since. The famed number one, the sixth prototype, is here at the Marshall Museum at our company headquarters. Pete Townshend loved the tone, but wanted it louder. He suggested a hundred-watt head on a single square 8 x 12 cab, but I told him it would be too heavy, and the roadies would complain. But we went ahead and built some for him anyway. Sheepishly, Pete had to agree that they were just too heavy to transport easily, so I ended up doing what I wanted to do in the first place, which was a 4 x 12 cab with a straight front with the angled one sitting on top, and that was how the stack was born.

Over the years, all of the top guitarists visited the shop, and all were special customers, but the one who stands out in my mind was James Marshall Hendrix. Jimi had played at Ronnie Scott's and wanted to play his Fender amp, but the stage was set up with a backline of Marshalls which could not be moved, so Jimi played through them and afterwards told Mitch he wanted to meet the man who had his name [on these amplifiers]! I of course knew Mitch — he was one of my drum pupils. So the next day Mitch brought Jimi to meet me at the shop, and this was the start of a great friendship. Jimi had a fantastic sense of humor, and I have long credited him as "Marshall's greatest ambassador."

Manny's Music store has a lot in common with Marshall Amplification, a family business that takes the time to look after and listen to what their loyal customers want — and has been instrumental to the birth and development of rock 'n' roll.

THE YOUNGBLOODS

RCA VICTOR RECORDS   WM. MORRIS AGENCY

Herbert S. Gart Management, Inc.

'61 W.54th Street   4502 Eighteenth Street

New Yo   N.Y. 100   San Francisco, Cal. 94114

(212)   1264   (415   863 - 6049

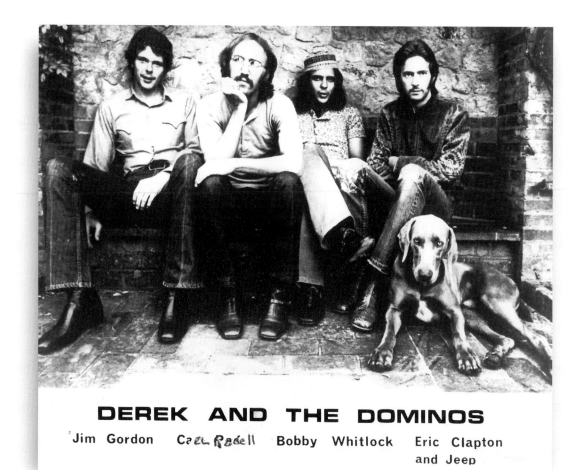

DEREK AND THE DOMINOS

Jim Gordon   Carl Radell   Bobby Whitlock   Eric Clapton
and Jeep

There was no way he was going to fit it all in a taxi to take him home.
At the time he was living by Lincoln Center, where the Chinese Embassy
used to be. I said to him, "Jimi, I am going to leave in a few minutes
with my brother-in-law, Mike Bergstein," who was there. Mike was an
insurance man, and not really into the music business. I told Jimi that
we'd drive him home with the gear in the Manny's van. We loaded up,
took everything to the hotel, and the doorman put all the stuff in his
room for him. We were driving away and my brother-in-law says, "Boy,
that's a weird looking guy. What an outfit he was wearing. He must be
a real whack ball." The next day Jimi Hendrix was on the cover of *Life*
magazine.

JANIS JOPLIN

PERS EMENT: AB◯/ INC./ALBERT B. GROSSMAN / BERT BLOCK /75 E. 55 N.Y.

"All his pickups were hot-wired so they were more powerful than normal. I was a pretty good guitar repairman, I knew how to fix Jimi's to make him happy."

Jimi enjoyed all his instruments, and he bought every guitar that was new. He bought a Rickenbacker 331, a psychedelic guitar — as you strummed it, the colors changed on the guitar. They called it "the light show guitar." It was really weird. But it never made it. Maybe he didn't use it. Usually any time a guitar came out that somebody like Hendrix used, or Jimmy Page, the sales of the guitars went up astronomically, because all the kids said, "If it's good enough for them, it's good enough for me." Page sold a lot of Les Pauls. Jimi Hendrix did more to sell Stratocasters than anybody. Hell, he was enormous to the guitar business. More than anyone I can think of, Jimi made Manny's a name among musicians.

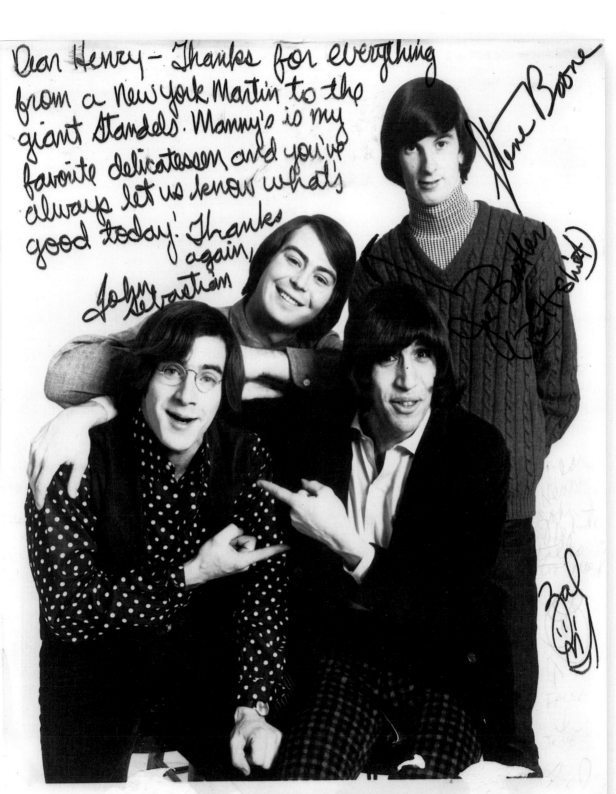

Dear Henry – Thanks for everything from a New York Martin to the giant Standels. Manny's is my favorite delicatessen and you've always let us know what's good today. Thanks again,
John Sebastian

Steve Boone

Joe Butler (& shirt)

Zal

LOVIN' SPOONFUL

"These guys can't even keep time."

My friendship with Henry began in 1962 or 1963. I was beginning to play around the Village, and mostly getting work playing harmonica. But guitar was really my main interest. I needed a serious guitar, so I went up to Manny's. I wanted a Gibson J-45. Downstairs would be the one that was out on the display, so that would be the only one you got to play. I went to Henry, and I said, "I know that there are a few more, but they're probably upstairs." Henry said, "John, don't bother me now. Come by at ten o'clock in the morning. Get up once in your life and I'll let you up into the stacks." Well, this was an amazing revelation. The next Tuesday I show up practically when they're rolling the front up, and Henry lets me into the stacks. I tell ya, I was in heaven that day.

I found the best J-45 that they put out. That guitar is on eighty percent of the Lovin' Spoonful's output. Every time there was an acoustic guitar, it's that guitar. Now what happened was I was working downtown, sweeping up in a guitar store, and I started realizing, "Gee, this guitar has a lot of finish on it. It has a lot more than we put on these classical guitars." So, in a moment of inspiration, at a time before there were collectors and people who would go, "Oh my God, you can't change that!" I took off the finish, slowly, with a German bedspring and some thinner — you know that German bedsprings are perfect for making a little edge that you curl around — and you can take the finish off. I came out with two handfuls of pink plastic off of that guitar. Now, it already was the best sounding guitar of the eight or ten that I had tried, but once I took the plastic off it and put a classical finish on it, just a regular lacquer, the thing roared.

Once the Spoonful got going, Zal Yanovsky said, "Okay, well, now I want to institute a rule: we only buy instruments from Henry. If we put all your eggs in that basket, we'll get better prices and the prices will keep getting better." So Zal's friendship with Henry was a very strong one.

It was Zali who first started to call the roadies "schleppers." It was a time when Jewish vernacular wasn't as out as it is now. You know, Hollywood made possible the inclusion of all of these different regional pasts, but specifically Yiddish. Hollywood has really made it more accessible to the world. At the time, though it really wasn't understood, so Zali had to explain to us that "schlepping" was "dragging a heavy object." It had a certain kind of a vibe to it. And then Henry started making the shirts.

I remember coming in to Manny's one late evening. The door wasn't shut, but the gates were coming down. And inside is this huge sound. And I came in through the door and I remember thinking, "You know, whoever it is, they're louder than Zali."

*Henry keeps an eye on
John Sebastian, circa 1966.*

And this took some doing. At that time we had the biggest things available to us, like Super Reverbs, and a Fender Bassman, which was loud, but not compared to a stack. So this was, I guess, the first of the Marshall stacks. I didn't know what they were, but Jimi Hendrix was trying them out. And of course he was trying it out on the crappy yellow Danelectro. It's true that every damn player in the neighborhood ended up on that guitar at one time or another. Why bring out a new guitar and let a guy scratch it up when all he wants to do is find out is whether a fuzz pedal works?

That was the thing. There was a feeling that you were collaborating with Henry. And nobody was putting pressure on you to buy one particular thing. The idea is to kind of find out what it is you're aiming for. 'Cause especially in the guitar world, these fine differences between a Telecaster and a Stratocaster become a huge deal. And you ask a player and he'll say, "It's a different instrument!" To have a little guidance was a big help.

When we got a picture on the wall, it was big. It was very big. And week to week we would be checking to find out if we were up. We'd been going, "Well, the Stones are up there now. These guys can't even keep time, and now they're big stars!"

Manny was the first white music salesman in Harlem.

Manny was my father. He was born in 1904 in New York City. He had a slight bit of musical knowledge, and he played a fair violin. In 1925, the year he married my mother, Jule, he went to work for Conn-Selmer Company. They were located at 117 West 48th Street. At that time, there were three stores in New York City: Wurlitzer, New York Band, and Conn-Selmer. Conn-Selmer went on to become one of the biggest manufacturers of brass instruments in the United States.

After two years on the job, as a commissioned salesman, he was making more money than the president, Joseph Greenfield. This annoyed so many of the Conn-Selmer executives that they transferred Manny to Hartford, Connecticut, to run their school music program.

He went with Jule and his new daughter, Helen, who was born in 1926. He was quite successful at this as well, and he decided that he did not need any more bosses. He took the family went back to New York City in 1935 and opened up a store right across the street from Conn and Selmer, at 120 West 48th Street.

The store at first was only about twenty feet by twenty feet, and since New York Band, Conn-Selmer, and Wurlitzer held all the franchises for the main instrument lines, he did not have that much to sell. And he couldn't get the school bands anymore because Conn-Selmer wouldn't sell him instruments.

Vincent Bach, a manufacturer of trumpets, took my father under his wing, and gave him ten or fifteen horns to put in his tiny front window, on the proviso that he could not sell them. All sales had to go

across the street to Bach's store, and Manny made a small commission. But with small accessories such as reeds and mutes, the store began to prosper. And he had the Gretsch drum company, and he made friends

with Bill Gretsch, who was the second president of Gretsch, after Fred Gretsch, Sr.

He decided that he couldn't make money selling to the schools, and the only thing that was really open was Harlem. So he went up to Harlem — he was the first white music salesman there. He made friends with all of the black musicians, friends who still, to this day, come into

Manny and Jules in the old store.
Above, Manny with Blue Note star J.J. Johnson.

the store and bless my father. He was the only guy who used to go up there and say, "Well, you don't have the money, pay me when you get a chance. Don't worry about it, I trust you." And then Manny's started to soar.

I have the original cashbook from those days. It shows sales of sixty-seven dollar saxophones that they paid off at two bucks a week. He sold to all of the big musicians, and they got to know and trust him. And my father began to discount the instruments. This was something that was never done by the other stores. Since musicians did not have much money, the word got around that they could buy cheaper at Manny's. My

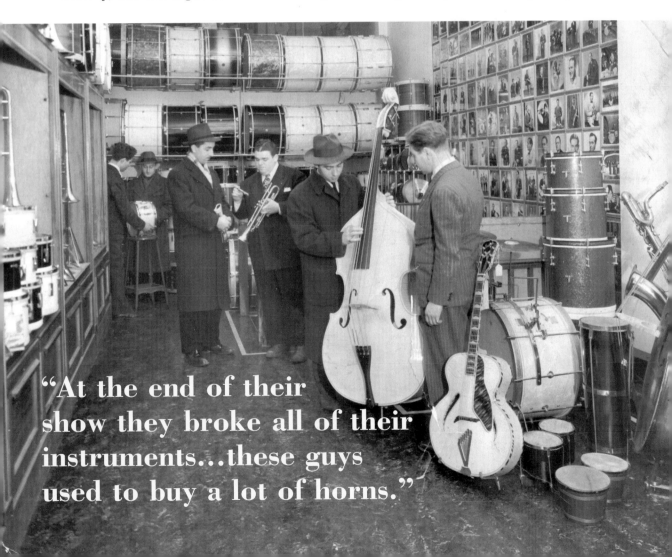

"At the end of their show they broke all of their instruments...these guys used to buy a lot of horns."

ELLA FITZGERALD
featured with
CHICK WEBB and His Orchestra

Personal Management
GALE Inc.
48 West 48th Street
New York

father issued credit to any musician working in a band at the big clubs and to the best of my knowledge, he never got stuck.

Ella Fitzgerald would come into the store when I was seven or eight years old, and take me out for malteds, and take me all around town. She used to watch after me like I was her own child. At the time she was singing with Chick Webb, the bandleader at the Apollo.

Chick Webb was a small, hunchbacked drummer, considered to be the best in the world, but since the clubs were run by mobsters, he never really got a salary commensurate with his talent. My father and the Gretsch family decided that the publicity of Chick playing Gretsch

"My father said he'd never seen a man so happy in his entire life."

drums would be worth more than the price of a drum set. The new set, in gold sparkle with little cut out chicks around the whole set, true old temple blocks, and old style cowbells, was quite a sight. They set the drums up at the Apollo and when Chick walked in, he cried like a baby. He walked on the stage that night and he saw this brand new drumset and he broke out hysterically. My father said he'd never seen a man so happy in his entire life. And he never forgot what Manny had arranged, and he made sure that all his musician friends shopped at Manny's.

My mother and father used to go up to Harlem all the time, and it was all run by gangsters in those days — Owney Madden, Dutch Schultz. My mother saw a guy get shot and then run over. Scenes like that were normal up in Harlem in those days.

When the white guys went up to Harlem, they usually wore white suits, and they were really always dapper. And the chairs were all rattan chairs, and if a guy was particularly nasty, the waiters would take damp teabags with long strings and take the string and swing the teabag under the chair. And then, when they got up, the back of their white pants would have this tea stain. My father used to tell that story many times. It was very embarrassing, because they'd walk out of the place and they didn't know what had happened to their pants.

I was born in 1932, and business was getting better and better. My first memories of the store are of cleaning up, carrying cartons. I was a little bit in awe if someone like Gene Krupa, or Benny Goodman, or Buddy Rich walked in. Sinatra used to come in when he was singing with the Dorsey Band.

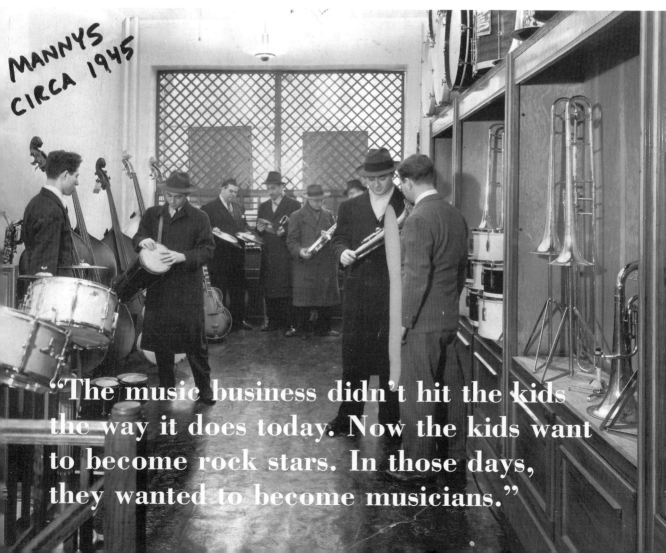

MANNYS CIRCA 1945

"The music business didn't hit the kids the way it does today. Now the kids want to become rock stars. In those days, they wanted to become musicians."

It's the Boogie Woogie

Fred Allen was a very good customer of ours. He was a very famous radio comedian and movie star, too. He and his wife Portland Hoffa did a weekly radio show that was more popular and more famous than the Jack Benny Show, but he died early on. He used to send me his scripts, so we'd listen to the radio with the scripts in our hand. That was fun.

By this time, Manny's was the meeting place for the all "the guys," along with Charlie's Tavern, the Shanghai Chinese, and Jim and Andy's, which was two doors down. Jim was the owner and Andy was his dog.

That's when we really started getting busy. During the late '30s and '40s, the big bands were unbelievable. And they used to buy like crazy.

Milt Hinton

"They always made us feel welcome, which is something not many whites, let alone store owners, did in those days."

The first time I was in Manny's was probably 1936 or 1937. I was in my late twenties, and I'd just come into New York with Cab Calloway's band. I remember the old store had two floors, and there were a couple of rehearsal studios above. Back in those days I already had one or two basses, so the only thing I was likely to buy at Manny's was a set of strings. I think the real reason I first got to Manny's had to do with some of my friends in Cab's band, like Ben Webster, Keg Johnson, and Foots Thomas, who used to spend hours at the store trying new instruments and talking about music.

Manny and Jule were wonderful people. They always made us feel welcome, which is something not many whites, let alone store owners, did in those days. We were all very aware of that. It's strange, you always hear about the after-hours places in the '30s and '40s, where black and white musicians hung out together all night. But at Manny's the same kind of thing went on during the day. I met guys like Doc Severinsen, Phil Bodner, and George Barnes in Manny's. They might be waiting to take a lesson at one of the studios across 48th Street, or maybe someone had a record date or a rehearsal on the block. Whatever it was, somehow we'd find ourselves hanging out in Manny's, and Manny and Jule didn't seem to mind at all.

Not only did Manny and Jule make black musicians feel comfortable, but they often gave blacks a chance to work a good job in the store itself. I remember Irene, a black woman

THE MODERN JAZZ QUARTET   ATLANTIC RECORDS

who seemed to be there from the start. Seeing a black woman with a respectable job like that was very unusual in those days, and we all felt great about it. I also remember Danny was in the drum department. And there was a black trombone player named Stompy who used to deliver instruments to guys on studio gigs or in rehearsal halls. Sometimes Manny and Jule even gave a summer job to a black musician's child. That's what happened to my friend Keg Johnson's son. The pay was good and I remember he even got his lunch included as part of the job.

Manny and his family were always willing to lend instruments to musicians — white or black, it didn't matter. The same thing was true about buying instruments on credit, and they were even known to have lent musicians cash from time to time.

I still remember the golf tournaments at the Engineers Country Club out on the Island. I don't know how the guest list was ever put together but there were always a great bunch of musicians in attendance. Once again there was an unusual mixture of black and white guys who often brought their wives to these events. There'd be celebrities like Sammy Davis, Joe Williams, Erroll Garner, but there'd also be regular guys like Tyree Glenn, Bucky Pizzarelli, Kelly Martin, Artie Ryerson, Osie Johnson. Playing golf seemed to be secondary to eating and drinking, which started early in the afternoon and ended in a jam session at dawn.

In the late '70s, '80s, and '90s, I worked less in Manhattan during the daytime so I didn't get into Manny's as often as when I was active in the studios. But whenever I got the chance I'd stop by the new store and see everyone. Of course, I remember Henry from the time he was in knee pants. Even as a kid he had the same warmth as his parents and he always made me feel as comfortable as they did.

As a musician working in New York for more than fifty years, Manny's was really a big part of my life. I met a lot of musicians in the store who became lifelong friends. I learned about the latest musical equipment, especially when amplification came in. And I got to know and love Manny and Jule who always made me feel like a part of their family.

It was nothing for a guy like Abe Lyman, who was a big band leader, to come out and hire five new guys and buy them all new instruments.

There was a band called Frank and Milt Britton — they were a comedy band. At the end of their show they broke all of their instruments. These were breakable instruments — they'd put them back together again at the end of the night. But something always happened. So these guys used to buy a lot of horns.

"During the late '30s and '40s, the big bands were unbelievable. And they used to buy like crazy.

When World War II broke out, the government made Manny head of the "office of musical instrument purchases." There was quite a bit of price gauging, due to the fact that metal was very scarce. The OPA, the Office of Price Administration, came to my father and said we need somebody downtown. They needed somebody to judge the price of musical instruments, so that when they bought for the Army bands they weren't taken over the hurdles. My father had that job.

After the War, we put a piano in the store, in the back. We had a guy working for us by the name of Nick Jerret. Nick's sister was Francis Wayne. Francis, at the time, was a singer with the Woody Herman band, very famous, and her husband was Neil Hefti, still a very famous name out in Hollywood. Nick put on these sessions, these great jam sessions. These sessions happened on union day — the music union opened on Wednesdays and Fridays from two o'clock until six o'clock. The jam sessions lasted for about two or three years until the police asked us to close it because drugs were being pushed. We didn't realize it.

It was like a safe house. Charlie Parker used to pass out. He'd go sleep

"by O'Brien"

COUNT BASIE

Exclusive Management:
Willard Alexander, Inc.
— *Artists Management*

660 madison avenue, new york city, new york 10021/plaza 1-7070
333 no. michigan avenue, chicago, illinois 60601/central 6-2460
315 so. beverly drive, beverly hills, calif. 90210/crestview 3-4322

NAT "KING" COLE
Personal Management: CARLOS GASTEL

GENERAL ARTISTS CORPORATION
NEW YORK   CHICAGO   BEVERLY HILLS   CINCINNATI
DALLAS   LONDON   MIAMI

all night long, on a couch upstairs. Howard McGee and Chet Baker died owing me God knows how much. Chet used to come in every week and borrow five dollars from me. Bud Powell came when he wasn't in the hospital on drugs. Miles Davis was very nice. All you've heard about Miles Davis, in those days he was as nice as could be, he was a perfect gentleman. Gerry Mulligan used to come in with Judy Holliday. She was a big movie star at the time. The music was great.

"Most of the great jazz musicians of the day came by Manny's to jam."

All the top players showed up — Dizzy Gillespie playing piano as well as trumpet, Charlie Parker playing tenor when his alto sax was unavailable, which usually meant he had pawned if for cash. Parker did not have much money, so Manny made a deal for him with the H. N. White-King band instrument company to supply him with a silver bell alto, for his endorsement. J. J. Johnson, Charlie Mingus, Thelonious Monk — most of the great jazz musicians of the day came by Manny's to jam. One of the great pictures on the wall is from Sonny Rollins. It is signed "To Manny's, where I bought my first horn…and many more after."

One day I was driving with my mother. I see Dizzy go by, and I beep the horn. And he stopped his car and he gets out, and he says, "I wouldn't get out of my car for anybody but your mother." They went back a lot of years. My father got him his first Martin trumpet with the upturned bill.

By 1946 we had bought the entire building, and we had two floors of studios upstairs. Benny Goodman had a little office up there. Popsie Randolph, who took photos of musicians, had a studio. We had a trum-

YOUNG MAN WITH A *Selmer* HORN

RAY ANTHONY

SAYS:

"My final choice is *Selmer*"

Photo above: Ray and his fine reed section, left to right. Ray Anthony—Trumpet, Jim Schneider—Alto, Bob Hardaway—Tenor, Earl Bergman—Alto, Billy Usselton —Tenor, Leo Anthony—Baritone using Selmer (Paris) saxophones and clarinets.

Voted the 1951 band of the year in Billboard Disc Jockey Poll, Ray Anthony plays the Selmer (Paris) Trumpet and fronts a 100% Selmer Reed section.

Hear Ray play his Selmer when he makes his next personal appearance in your vicinity, on the air, or on his new Capitol recordings.

Hear how much better you'll sound with a new model Selmer (Paris) Trumpet, Saxophone or Clarinet—ask your local dealer to arrange a free trial. Or, write for free literature to Selmer Dept. B-11

Photo above: Leo Anthony backs up Ray with his new Selmer Super-Action Baritone Saxophone.

H. & A. **Selmer** INC.
ELKHART, INDIANA

pet player by the name of Lamar Wright and a saxophone player by the name of Eddie Barefield. They both played with Cab Calloway. We had a guitarist, Hy White, who played in the Woody Herman band and wrote a famous guitar method book. Lots of guys had teaching studios. And that's how the building progressed until 1953 or '54, when we took over the whole building for storage.

Artie Shaw

In 1964 or '65, the Rockefellers started coming to us to buy our building. But my father would never sell. This went on and on and on, and they finally made us an offer we couldn't refuse. And we took their offer — and it was a very good one. They bought us a new building just down the street (and they were giving us a substantial amount of money, too), and built us a new building, to our specifications. They took over our old building, and ripped it down.

When we went into the new building, of course there were problems. The builder had made a lot of money on the deal and he just left. He just took off, leaving us with tons of problems. The Rockefellers came in and did everything we asked. They were very honorable about it. They

"Who killed this bear back here?"

My father, Manny, loved musicians; he loved the kids. He always said that because of learning music and learning different styles and composers, they were more educated than a lot of people who went to school.

When I hit sixteen, I started working in the store in the summers. I would have paid my father to go to work there. My father used to say it got too exciting — when rock 'n' roll became big, there wasn't enough time to talk to any of the musicians any more.

Later, Henry ran the store with my husband, Danny, who built up the percussion department. He played the drums, and he was the only one who knew the difference between a marimba and a xylophone! When the drums came into the store for the Beatles, girls would come and slip notes into them. They'd see the Ludwig boxes and leave

notes for Ringo. It was cute. He taught Ringo how to use an electric tom-tom that Ludwig had sent down.

Henry knew all the guitar players. He was their age and they all got along. The Lovin' Spoonful, Paul Simon, the Who — everyone liked and respected Henry. He worked hard. He never let anyone bug the stars for autographs. And he had a lot of good help at Manny's. I stopped working there in 1991, but I've seen it all! I remember George Benson playing, and a bunch of guitar players hanging out and saying, "Hey, he's good. He's gonna make it."

I remember Frank Zappa threw his fur coat on the floor, and Henry said, "Who killed this bear back here?" It was a big coat.

Freak Out: Aunt Helen (above) takes on Frank Zappa and the Mothers.

50

were very straight-ahead people.

That's how we got the building where we are now at 156 W.48th Street. We moved there officially in 1969. My father never got to see it.

My father was in the right place at the right time. He was very smart. He knew what he was doing. He was so well liked by the musicians that they went out of their way. Even though by the late '40s and '50s there were a lot of stores in New York City, Manny's was always the predominant music store in New York.

"Hey, you have to take care of yourself."

Manny's was my first job in New York. My brother Billy and I came from Elmira, in the western part of the New York state. Tommy was already in the city doing the fashion thing.

Billy went to Manny's to get a job, and Henry said, come tomorrow if you're serious. So Billy got there early and waited for them to open, and Henry hired him on the spot as a stock boy. And he said if your brother wants a job, tell him to come on down. This was 1983, I was like twenty-three years old.

Henry liked the Hilfiger kids. He promoted Billy to guitar salesman, and Billy dealt with all the rock stars because he had such a great personality.

Henry's kids came in one day and said, "Hey, we bought some of your brother Tommy's shirts over at Saks Fifth Avenue." We said, "Sure, he's a designer." And they said, "Yeah, but his shirts were with Polo, and the expensive, nice, preppy shirts!"

Tommy said, "I could be the next Calvin Klein," but we didn't care about that, we just wanted to play guitars. A few days later in Times Square there was a billboard that said "The four great American designers are CK, RL, PE, and the newest, TH." That's Calvin Klein, Ralph Lauren, Perry Ellis, and Tommy. Henry saw it and said, "Hey, is that your brother's billboard?"

Billy became Henry's right-hand man, dealing with Bowie and Jagger and everyone, and I left because I didn't want to be a stock boy anymore. Billy had brain cancer and died in 2001. He was like Henry's other son. That day, I called Henry in Florida, and he broke down and cried.

Henry was like our father. If we came in from being out all night, he'd say, "Hey, you have to take care of yourself." He was strict, but respectful. He had that smile. He helped us grow. He really helped us with our careers. I learned the whole entertainment business being in Manny's. I learned how to deal with people. I learned the bullshit. We were green when we came to New York.

Andy Hilfiger is the senior vice president of marketing for Tommy Hilfiger and a partner, with Jennifer Lopez, in Sweetface Fashion.

Andy's boss.

> **"And these guys loved music. When they got done working, they wanted to play more and they wanted to be with their peers. How do you think all those after-hours clubs got started?"**

We always took good care of professional musicians. In fact in, 1951, or 1952, the Musicians Union Local 802 moved downtown to Allen Street, in the Lower East Side. So my father opened up a small store on Forsythe Street. The store was tiny, but it had the reeds for the guys who came down there, the men who belonged to Local 802. He opened that store just to cater to musicians. That was our stock and trade.

And these guys loved music. When they got done working, they wanted to play more and they wanted to be with their peers. How do you think all those after-hours clubs got started? Today, these guys, when they get done playing, they don't want to be with their peers, they want to go home.

We always had the youngsters in the store, but it wasn't that open. The music business didn't hit the kids the way it does today. Now the kids want to become rock stars. In those days, they wanted to become musicians. It's a whole different thing. People used to be in the business because they loved music.

BUDDY HOLLY   BRUNSWICK RECORDS   GENERAL ARTISTS CORPORATION   MANAGEMENT:
&
THE CRICKETS   NEW YORK · CHICAGO · BEVERLY HILLS · CINCINNATI · DALLAS · MIAMI BEACH · LONDON   ORMAN PETTY

A lot of guys would just take any guitar. Most of them didn't know the difference. But Buddy knew. He checked them all.

Buddy Holly had Gerry Allison and Joe B. Maudlin in his band. Waylon Jennings didn't come until later. Gerry Allison, the drummer, used to drive us crazy. He'd come into the store and try everything, banging the drumsticks on the wooden counters. Joe was very quiet. And Buddy himself was very humble, he never said, "Hey, I'm Buddy Holly." We became very friendly. In fact, when Judi and I got engaged,

Fender fine electric instruments

1954 CATALOG

Wildwood Series: Coronado II with tremolo, Wildwood Acoustic with pickup, Coronado II Bass, Coronado 12-string—foreground, two Wildwood Acoustics.

Coronado Series: Coronado I with tremolo, Coronado II with tremolo, Coronado 12-string, Coronado I Bass, Coronado II Bass.

Solid-State Amp Series: Super/Reverb, Twin/Reverb, Pro/Reverb., Vibrolux/Reverb, Bassman, Deluxe/Reverb.

GREAT **NEW** SOUND

SAME **OLD** QUALITY

Fantastic customized, one-of-a-kind WILDWOOD guitars; new expanded Coronado Series guitars and basses; the new improved Fender Solid-State Series amps; all these and many more for 1967!

MUSICAL INSTRUMENTS

SANTA ANA, CALIF.

Once Again, Comparison Will Prove Fender's Superiority

See them at the Fender display at the 1967 NAMM Show, June 25-29, North Hall and Rms. 545, 546, 547 & 549, Hilton Hotel, Chicago, Ill.

"For amplifiers, whatever we had that was loud, he took. He wasn't so particular."

he sent us a fifteen-dollar check for a wedding gift.

When he first started coming in he was buying Stratocasters. He loved white Stratocasters. He also bought a bunch of acoustics. He later went into Guilds, but mostly the Gibsons — the J-200 and the Hummingbird. But he tried out everything to make sure that it suited him.

For amplifiers, whatever we had that was loud, he took. He wasn't so particular about his amplification. He liked his guitars, he had his style. He didn't really care as much about the amplifiers. I don't even remember what he used to buy exactly, but I'm sure it was Fender amps.

Years later, after Buddy died, I was driving on Riverside Drive with my wife, and a guy cuts me off. Pulls me over. I said, "Whatsa matter?" He said, "You're Henry, aren't you, from Manny's?" He said, "You were at Buddy Holly's wedding?" I said, "No." He said, "I thought you were at Buddy Holly's wedding." I said, "No, I was invited, but couldn't make it." "You knew Buddy Holly? What kind of guy was he like?" "He was a good friend, he was a nice guy." I asked, "Why?" He said, "My name is Don McLean, and I'm writing a song about him. It's called 'American Pie.'"

Don McLean

"More like a delicatessen than a music store!"

I bought my first Martin guitar at Manny's, a D-28 1963 vintage, which was later stolen at the Newport Folk Festival. I used it for the first half of my first album, *Tapestry*. The remainder of the record was completed with a replacement D-28 also purchased at Manny's in 1969, with money given to me by Pete and Toshi Seeger out of the goodness of their hearts, since I was broke and I was singing with Pete at Newport when the original guitar was swiped.

Since I was not a New Yorker, I was struck by the furious activity at Manny's. It was not unlike the stock exchange on Wall Street, everyone shouting quotes and running around. There were lots of yelling, which I was also not used to coming from the tree-lined, quiet streets of suburbia as I did.

Henry, you were a good yeller and a hard worker. You were always talking with everyone and cutting deals, and boxes of everything were being moved constantly under your direction. You did have a wonderful ability to remember people and connect with them, but best of all, you always came through with the best price!

What made Manny's different from any other store is that it's really more like a delicatessen than a music store! I think my first publicity photo was put up in 1971, there were others after that, and from time to time over the years I have come to Manny's to see how it has

changed and to look at myself and see how I have changed and to be proud of all the great company I have on those walls.

I remember pulling up next to you at a tollbooth on the Westside Highway, rolling down my window and asking you if you knew Buddy Holly. You said you did — you can guess what my mind was working on!

Don McLean

Herbert S. Gart Management, Inc.
35 W. 53 St., Suite 53
New York, New York 10019
(212) 765-8160

58

Manny, Great pleasure
dealing with you
Sincerely
Bill Haley

Rudy
Pedro
GAC

Billy

Rolly

Al

John

BILL HALLEY & THE COMETS

The famous yellow guitar.

I was not known for having the nicest personality in the music business.

When Buddy Holly came in, nobody ever went up to him and annoyed him. When the Beatles came in, nobody bugged 'em. Everyone knew better. And if they did, I would kick 'em out of the store. And if you weren't going to buy anything, you weren't going to hang around the store trying everything. I used to tell everyone, You try it, you buy it. We don't have any "tryouts" here. That's how the yellow guitar got started. Everybody wanted to try out an amplifier or an effect, and I did not want them to try with a new guitar. Most of these kids would scratch it with their belt buckle or something.

One day somebody was doing a photo shoot here, and they had a bunch of instruments that they had painted colors: a trombone painted pink, a drum set painted in black. They had this Danelectro guitar painted in yellow. I bought five or six of these painted instruments, maybe twenty bucks for the whole bunch, and I put the yellow guitar on the floor. I decided that when anyone came in to try an instrument, an amplifier, or a sound device, we would use this show guitar. I told everybody that I had hot-wired the pickups, which I never did. It just happened to be a super guitar.

And everybody played it — Hendrix, McCartney, Harrison, Clapton. They all used this guitar. If they said they wanted to play something else, forget it. I didn't get any crap from those guys. If these guys wanted to use a Stratocaster, I'd say, no this is a better guitar. And they never really argued with me. They all knew me, they knew my father. So they listened. And this guitar was unbelievable.

That guitar had to have been played by more famous guitarists… I remember one day, Jerry Garcia, Bob Dylan, Bob Weir, Joe Cocker — there were like six rock stars, superstars, passing the guitar around, just sitting around playing it.

"Everybody played it — Hendrix, McCartney, Harrison, Clapton. They all used this guitar."

George Harrison wanted to buy it. I wouldn't sell it to him. He said, "I'll give you $200 for it."

"I'm not gonna sell it, George."

"But I love this guitar!"

I never sold it. If it wasn't such a good luck charm, I might have. He was really bummed over that. This guitar belongs in the Hall of Fame — it was probably played by more musicians than any other instrument in the world. Every guitarist that came in that wanted to try an effect, had to use the yellow guitar.

The Rolling Stones came in in 1966, and I showed them the Gibson Maestro Fuzz-Tone, which had just arrived. Mick Jagger said to me, "I could put a hole in my speaker, get the same sound." "Yeah," I told him, "Now you've got a hole in the speaker and you've got to repair the speaker. Just try it." They tried it, and they used it on "Satisfaction." That's the first record that it was used on. Mick Jagger bought one of

JOE COCKER - BIG WILLIE

Press: D. McNally
(415) 648-4832

GRATEFUL DEAD
1989
G.D. Productions
Box 1073
San Rafael, CA 94915

Photo: Ken Friedman

the first ones. I sold it to him.

The Fuzz-Tone was huge. Unbelievable. When you talk about things that made an impact, it was amazing. We could never keep them in stock. And then everybody came out with different ideas. There were so many companies with different effects.

I wanted a fuzz-tone with my own sound. So I had this guy, Mike Matthews, make me up a fuzz-tone with a Manny's fuzz. And in fact on the picture in the store from Jimi Hendrix, it says, "You always want me to talk about your fuzz-tone." Our fuzz-tone was really a completely different-sounding unit. It was fuzzier!

The next year, Vox introduced the Wah-Wah pedal, and they took me and a couple of my employees down to their showroom. I'll tell you, it knocked us all for a loop. I think it was the most popular effect ever. And I don't know who bought the first one, but once we got 'em in, we couldn't keep 'em in stock. Hundreds of other things took off because of that – phase shifters, flangers, you name it.

Vox was a very clever company. They came out with their Vox Continental organ. A great organ – if you knew how to repair it. And their amplifiers, the Super Beatle, and the Royal Guardsman – great sounds, but they were constantly in the repair shop. The AC-30 was very popular. Great amp, but they were very self-destructive. Then they tried to come up with a guitar line, but that went flop.

They really had a lot of problems. A lot of companies were like that. Magnatone was the first one to go with this weird vibrato. Everybody

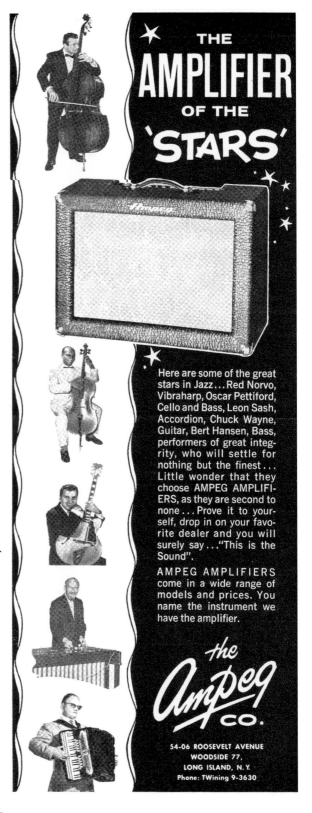

Electrifying Opportunity:

Vox Ampliphonic.

Here's the next big trend in the music business. Vox Ampliphonic will go like guitars. It may be even bigger.

Vox Ampliphonic is an exclusive new line of electronically equipped band instruments, amplified music stands, electronic pickups, stereo Multi-Voice tone divider and sound accessories. They're from the leader in electronic music — Vox. Only Vox could have come up with a system so accurate and so dependable.

Vox Ampliphonic lets the musician duplicate any recording studio sound — anywhere! It gives the horn player a place in the new-beat combos. It lets the musician play relaxed,

without being drowned out — yet still come through with the natural sound of the instrument. It puts an unheard-of variety of new sounds at the player's fingertips. Vox Ampliphonic — a profitable new sales opportunity for the music dealer. And sales are *over the counter sales.* Direct from dealer to musician.

VOX *ampliphonic*

Get with Vox. For franchise information write: Vox Ampliphonic, Box P1067, 8345 Hayvenhurst Avenue, Sepulveda, California 91343.

BIG BROTHER & THE HOLDING COMPANY

PERSONAL MANAGEMENT: ABC/M INC./ALBERT B. GROSSMAN/JOHN COURT/75 E. 55 ST., N.Y.C.

had a tremolo, which varies the volume, but this was the only amp to have true vibrato, which varies the pitch. Fender never had it, even though they call their amps "Vibrolux." It is just tremelo. The Maganatone had a different, sweeter sound. And that made it very popular. But Magnatone never took off as a company. They didn't do everything they were supposed to do to be successful. They never had the all-around great sounds that were Fender. They were good, but they were never great.

Ampeg made great amplifiers. Of course they started out with the

bass amplifier. The B-15 Portaflex, which is the one that you opened the cover, and the amp section sat on top of the cabinet, was their number-one seller. For guitars, the Jet was the most popular, that was the small one. It sold for under one hundred bucks. It was very popular. The Geminis came after. The Reverberocket was one that was really a boon to them, because it added reverb in a combo amplifier, and I think that was the first one that did it. Reverb was still a relatively unknown thing. That came in right after the vibrato, and it really changed the sound of the guitar player. And then every company tried to emulate it, and very few could do it.

The Marshall stack was the most popular of all amplifiers. They were huge, even before Jimi Hendrix used them at Woodstock, but that really put them over the top. The Who had been buying lots of them. Of

68

THE MAMAS & THE PAPAS   EXCLUSIVELY ON **DUNHILL**

Jack Casady

"Beyond any of the rock-star stuff…"

When the Jefferson Airplane was coming to New York regularly, from 1967 on, after Bill Graham opened the Filmore East, Manny's was the place where we did all of our shopping. We had a great relationship with Henry. He had a wry sense of humor. He would never take any of us seriously. He was beyond any of the rock star stuff. We're East Coasters, Jorma and me are both from Washington, so we weren't just these crazy Californians, we related well. And I'm a jazz fan and I loved seeing those great players photos on the walls. It was like a big toy store. Everyone wanted to go to Manny's.

He would give us great credit, which we'd try not to abuse. But like all musicians, sometimes we needed stuff and he'd let it go for a while, which made a huge difference. And this went on year after year. Manny's was a very personable place. We knew Henry's wife, and we watched his daughter Holly grow. I love Henry. He is a people person, and has such empathy about him. When I came in he'd practically crush me with a bear hug. He's helped so many musicians — everyone who came through New York.

Jorma Kaukonen

"I may still owe him money!"

I first went to Manny's sometime in the mid-to late '60s. I was with the Jefferson Airplane at the time, and our thing was just starting to happen. I'm thinking that my friend Larry Coryell told me about Manny's? In any case, at that time it was the largest most complete guitar store I had ever seen. We take megastores for granted these days, but back then Manny's was a real eye-opener. I doubt that I would have had either the money or the credit to buy anything the first time I visited 48th Street, but in those days we were just encouraged to look at stuff and hang out.

So many things were purchased there, once we started to have play money. I bought my Orange amplifier stacks as well as my Hi watts there.

Many of the Gibson guitars that were onstage mainstays for Hot Tuna in the '70s were purchased there. More outboard gear, strings and other such, were also purchased there. I don't think that a Jefferson Airplane recording from the late '60s onward was made without some piece of equipment from Manny's. I know that Manny's gear was present at almost every Hot Tuna session.

When we first got our picture up on the wall, it was an honor. We may still be up there somewhere, still young and bright-eyed. You would always meet fellow musicians there. When the English guys would come to town, you could almost count on running into them browsing through the stacks of gear. I remember seeing

Ready for takeoff: Jack (top) and Jorma (far right) in Airplane days.

Pete Townshend there, as well as countless others whose names are now lurking somewhere in the back of my murky memory.

I am on the seventy side of sixty now and as I look back, I will tell you what made Manny's so special to me. In the '80s, when I set about dismantling my life, I was no longer so concerned with taking care of business. No matter how tardy I was with payment, Henry never refused me something that I needed. I may still owe him money! I don't know. Henry was always a mensch to me. There is no praise higher than that for a man. Henry, may you live long and continue to smile!

CONVERTIBLE

ACOUSTIC/ELECTRIC. As a non-electric, this model produces clear sustained tones. The special pickup kit may be added if and when desired, to convert to electric guitar. Simple installation. Predrilled holes have decorative inserts.

GUITAR WITHOUT PICKUP . . . Uses standard Danelectro neck. Fully adjustable bridge.

Blonde Model 5005 .... $45

PICKUP KIT includes all controls and 10 ft. cord. Especially designed for Model 5005 guitar. Not for use with any other make or model. Model 9010 .... $20

GUITAR WITH PICKUP . . . Same as 5005 with Pickup 9010 completely assembled at the factory. May be used with or without amplification.

Blonde Model 5015 .... $65

Hard Shell Case No. 9842 30
or
Zippered Canvas Bag No. 9800 10

GUITARLIN

This new instrument is a guitar with fingerboard extended deep into the body. 31 frets combine the guitar and mandolin range. Tuned and played as a guitar with regular guitar strings. Guitar tone in lower register shades to mandolin in upper register.

Bronze Sunburst Model 4123 $150
Hard Shell Case No. 9842 30

LONG HORN BASS

Continued refinements have resulted in a superb instrument. Used in many recent recordings, T.V. programs and motion pictures. Available in two models, 4 string or 6 string, in bronze and white sunburst.

4 STRING BASS Model 4423 $150
6 STRING BASS Model 4623 150
Hard Shell Case No. 9842 30

DOUBLE NECK

Guitar and bass. Compact thin body design, overall size 17½" x 39" is smaller than some concert model guitars. Separate tone and volume controls for each neck. Three way switch connects either neck alone or both together. All frets within easy reach. White sunburst.

DOUBLE-NECK Model 3923 .... $175
HARD SHELL CASE Model 9943 35

SPECIAL STRINGS

Bass Strings — 29½" Scale. Fits Models A1B4, C2B4, C2B6, D2B4, D2B6.

Set of 4: GDAE	No. 940	$5.50
Set of 6: EBGDAE	No. 960	7.50
Individually		
E (high)	No. 901	$1.00
B	No. 902	1.00
G	No. 903	1.00
D	No. 904	1.00
A	No. 905	2.00
E (low)	No. 906	2.00

Flat Wound Bass Strings — 33½" Scale. Fits Model E2N4.

Set of 4: GDAE	No. 840	$13.70
Individually		
G	No. 803	$2.30
D	No. 804	2.80
A	No. 805	4.00
E	No. 806	4.60

12 String Guitar String Packet

Set of 12 plus 5 Spares. Fits all Danelectro 12 String Guitars	No. 917	$7.50

course Pete Townshend broke many of them, smashing his guitar into the cabinets. I know he had to re-cone a lot of speakers.

When they started it was based somewhat on the Fender Bassman, which was Fender's most popular amp at the time. Guitar players loved it. The Bassman had four speakers, but it was miniscule compared to the Marshall. Jim Marshall was a good friend to Manny's — he came to New York many times to push his amplifiers. He had to give away a lot at the beginning. And then of course he didn't have to give anything away.

"Our fuzz-tone was really a completely different sounding unit. It was fuzzier!"

In my opinion, Gibson never made a good amplifier. The only amplifier they made that was good was their stereo amplifier. They had one that was in the triangular shape, and that was a good amp. And if a guy had a Gibson stereo guitar, the ES-345, that was a great-sounding unit put together. Except for the Fuzz-Tone, they never had a good accessory department. But they tried.

Unfortunately, when the Norlin Industries took over Gibson in 1969, they destroyed the company. That's when Norton Stevens came in. He was from one of the textile companies, I think. He didn't know any-thing about guitars or music. First thing he did was sell out the horn business — they had Reynolds, they had Olds — they got rid of those two companies. They got rid of everything they could, so they could drop the company and sell it for a loss. They ended up running a lot of debt and really ruining the brand. Then Henry Juszkiewicz came in in the early '80s, and he fired everybody in the company, everybody. He kept nobody, and put his own people in. He bought things that nobody ever thought he should buy, made things that nobody ever thought he should

GIBSON AMPLIFIERS

THE CUSTOM-BUILT AMPLIFIER—GA-CB

The result of years of electronic and acoustical research by Gibson engineers, the Custom-Built Amplifier is superlative in electronic sound reproduction and has the tremendous volume and tone qualities found only in the finest public address broadcasting systems. The luggage-type case has detachable back and sturdy handle; Levelmatics on the base assure correct floor balance.

Other GA-CB features: Jensen's finest 15" Coaxial Speaker has

50 to 15,000 Cycle range; 30 to 40 watt output; ten tubes; adjustable built-in Tremolo; 3 controlled plug-in jacks and separate microphone jack; size—26" long, 12" wide, 20½" high; weight 60 pounds. This top model in Gibson's complete amplifier line has been acclaimed for use in studio work, for churches and auditoriums.

GA-CB Amplifier (Inc. Cover)......$425.00

GA-30 AMPLIFIER

A new member of the Gibson amplifier family is the beautifully styled GA-30 model, encased in dark brown leatherette, and designed to give the player a large choice of unusual performance effects.

Twin Jensen 12" and 8" speakers offer true fidelity of tone

in both high and low registers; full 14 watt output allows an extra wide range of volume and tone colors; 6 tubes are used in the special tone control circuit of the GA-30, which has 4 input jacks and separate tone and volume controls.

New bass Tone Expander control allows the player to increase resonance and quality of the lower notes, advantageous in instrumental solo work.

GA-30 Amplifier...$139.50
30C Cover for Above Amplifier...$ 5.25

GA-75 AMPLIFIER

An outstanding amplifier, the GA-75 offers unusual tone response and performance. For ease of operation and adjustment of controls, the chassis is mounted at the top of the case.

The GA-75 has 7 tubes, 15" speaker capable of 25 watt output, an acoustically treated speaker baffle, specially designed duo-tone control circuit with separate controls for bass and treble tone, control panel is removable for easy servicing. A special feature of the GA-75 is the 5 input jacks . . . 4 instruments and 1 microphone, each jack independent of the others with no interaction between instruments. This amplifier has proven ideal for accordion and string bass amplification.

The luggage-type case is covered with brown leatherette; size—24" wide, 20" high and 9½" deep; weight—28 pounds.

GA-75 Amplifier (Inc. Cover).........................$212.50

NOTE: Maximum wattage output is achieved in all GIBSON AMPLIFIERS,
due to the high grade speakers used in all models.

JOE WALSH

WARNER BROS.

Photo Credit: Henry Diltz

make, and now he's doing fantastic. Gibson is back on top.

And when CBS took over Fender in 1965, they ruined the guitars. The quality control was horrendous. But when Bill Schultz came in, Fender became very viable again, because he loved guitars. He was president of Yamaha, and then he took over Fender in 1985, and made Fender a gigantic company again. He took it from CBS, bought it for nothing, and made the company probably the biggest company in the business today. They are fantastic, and he's a fantastic leader. He was a very smart businessman. He took the company, moved it out of Fullerton,

"George Harrison wanted to buy it. I wouldn't sell it to him."

California, where everything was so expensive, and moved manufacturing to other places in the world, and to other places in the United States. He knew what he was doing and he did it right. When CBS took it over, their equivalent guitars were not good. Everything was on a downgrade. It's the same thing that happened to Gibson when Norlin took it over. These big companies took over just to dump them later and make some money.

There were a few other guitar companies that I liked that had different approaches. Semie Mosely started in the business with nothing. He came to New York in the early '60s with this guitar, the Moserite, and it had the thinnest neck on an instrument I've ever seen. It was very different. He got the Ventures to sign up with him. At that time the Ventures were pretty big. Good guitar players.

He came out with this guitar, and I asked him to take the line on. And it was a hard sell at first, but after a while people got used to the thin-

GO OVER BIG WITH MARSHALL

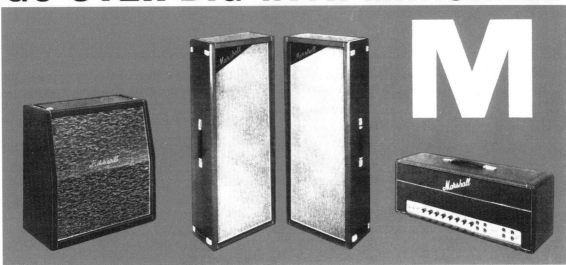

M

Famous Groups using Marshall Equipment:

ROY ORBISON	MARK LEEMAN FIVE	SMALL FACES
WHO	THE SECOND THOUGHTS	LULU & THE LUVVERS
SPENCER DAVIS	EDEN KANE	VAGABONDS
THE MOODY BLUES	THE YARDBIRDS	GRAHAM BOND ORGANISATION
IVY LEAGUE	TONY RIVERS AND THE	THE ACTION
CLIFF BENNET AND THE	CASTAWAYS	GARY FARR & THE T-BONES
REBEL ROUSERS	THE CHEROKEES	
THE NEXT FIVE	PETERS FACES	

ness of the neck and the speed of the neck; it became very popular. Never as big as any Fender or Gibson, but it was a popular instrument. He was an inventive guy. Great designs.

The guy that owned Rickenbacker had a lot of innovative ideas. They made good guitars, and basses, too. The 4001 bass was a huge seller. His name was John Hall, and it was his way or no way, and if you didn't go his way, he wouldn't sell to you. He was a very tough guy, very cold. He ran that company with a steel hand. If he didn't like you, he took the line away from you. If you did something wrong, he wouldn't sell you. If he didn't like what you did that week, he'd slow-ship you the popular models. He was tough. One day he decided he wanted to hold the price of his guitars at retail — we weren't allowed to discount. Of course we did anyway. He found out and he got very angry, said he was gonna pull the line from me. So I doubled my order. He didn't pull the line.

Nat Daniels lived down in Neptune, New Jersey. And he decided he

A Sign of Quality

beyond comparison...

mosrite
® OF CALIFORNIA INC.

1424 " P" STREET, BAKERSFIELD, CALIFORNIA

was going become a very rich man on a very cheap guitar. This was the late '50s, early '60s. So he made these Danelectro guitars. They were made from cheap wood with actual lipstick covers on his pick-ups. They used to cost $49 or $50, and we sold 'em for about $69, $70. But musicians, the real musicians, loved his six-string bass, which Fender later copied and made the Fender VI, which was never as popular. Every professional musician had to have a Danelectro six-string bass.

And then Nat Daniels quit the business and moved to Hawaii. He had

"The Marshall stack was the most popular of all amplifiers. They were huge, even before Jimi Hendrix used them at Woodstock."

something like eighty or ninety of these six-string basses left, and I bought every one of them. I think we paid thirty or forty bucks for them and sold them for $150 each. It was on a lot of records. It was a very popular thing.

Same thing with Ampeg, when they were run by Everett Hull. He made this thing called a "Baby Bass," which was a solid-body bass, very thin, shaped like a bass, but about half-width, and played like a stand-up. And every Latin player had to have one of these. We sold unbelievable quantities, and it wasn't cheap. I think it was $300 or $400 in those days, and then Everett died, and they sold out to one of the big companies. But I bought all the Baby Basses they had, I think maybe twenty of them. And we made a good profit on that one. That was, and it still is, among the Latin-American players, extremely popular. I'm sure every band has one of these. And they made hundreds of copies of them, but nothing ever compared to the Baby Bass. It was quite an instrument.

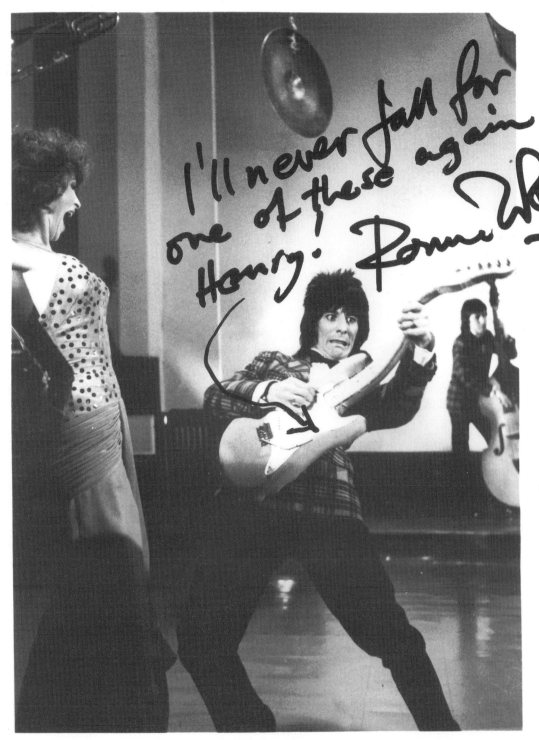

I'll never fall for
one of these again
Henry. Ronnie Wood

(c) '84 Ken Regan - Camera 5

Ron Wood

Rolling Stones Records

KENNY ROGERS and THE FIRST EDITION

When Elvis hit in '56, folk music was also very big.

Pete Seeger, the Highwaymen, the Weavers. In fact, Gil Robbins, one of the guys in The Highwaymen, was a very dear friend of mine, and used to bring his family to hang out at my house. His son is Tim Robbins, the actor, who comes in all the time. One time he came in the store with Susan Sarandon, and he asked me, "Do you remember the time we went

JUDY COLLINS

THE NEW WORLD SINGERS
ATLANTIC RECORDS

to your house? I guess I was seven or eight." It was my mother-in-law's house, a gigantic home up in Nyack. It had an unreal swimming pool — cold, ice water — and we used to throw firecrackers, the big bombers, into the pool. He remembered that.

Before the Beatles, of course Elvis was the thing. I first heard Elvis when I was in the Army, in Fort Smith, Arkansas, on my way to Korea. I went overseas, I'm in Korea, I'm in Okinawa, and all of the sudden you start to hear all of this country music. I came home and went to work in the store in '56, and Elvis was huge. He was a customer of ours, and his guitar player, Jimmy Burton, always came into the store. But for Elvis Presley to go out on the street, it was impossible. One day I got a phone call, "This is Elvis Presley." I laughed. I didn't believe him, we got prank calls all the time. He said, "I'm staying at the Waldorf, and I have a problem, I need some strings and two cables." I was going to go, but I didn't think it was professional for the boss to be making deliveries. So we sent it up with one of the kids who worked here. I think the bill was

"One day I got a phone call, 'This is Elvis Presley.'"

thirty-something dollars, and Elvis gave the kid a fifty-dollar tip. He really was a gentleman. But he never walked into the store. Of all the famous rock stars that there were, he was the biggest. But he never came in. And he never gave us a photo.

The folk thing was a craze like you wouldn't believe — Peter, Paul & Mary; the Rooftop Singers; the New Christie Minstrels; Kenny Rogers was in a group called the First Edition. Banjos and folk guitars were the thing. After the banjo craze, there was the pedal steel craze. I used to buy fifty, seventy-five pedal steels a week — a week! Couldn't keep them in the store. I used to sell ten a day. We were the only ones in New York City that carried pedal steels. The Sho-Bud was very popular. Nashville was getting big, and now every guy in New York had to play pedal steel. Now you can hardly find a pedal steel in Nashville. But it was a big thing, pedal steel.

And it was amazing, the amount of banjos we sold. There was a banjo called the Ne Plus Ultra, and on the side of the banjo they had a little wah-wah type handle that changed the sound. It was a really incredible thing, just gorgeous, one of the most ornate banjos ever made. I had a

Dion DiMucci

"A date with Marilyn Monroe..."

I've known Henry for six decades — I was fifteen when I bought my first new Gibson at Manny's in 1955. When I received my first royalty check, in 1957, for "Teenager in Love" going gold, I got on the first D train from Fordham Road in the Bronx to downtown 48th Street. I had my eye on the J-200 they had on display for $350. I still have it.

I had two fantasies when I was a kid — one was to have my own Martin D-28, like Hank Williams — the other was to have a date with Marilyn Monroe. Only one of those would come true. Henry was never able to come up with her phone number. But we're still good friends!

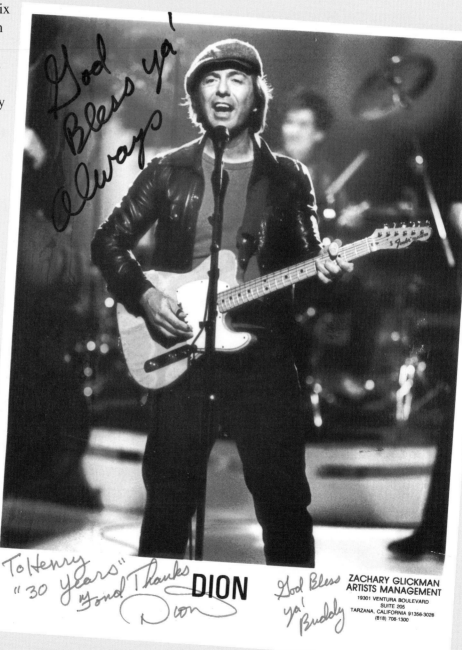

God Bless ya' Always

To Henry "30 Years" "Fond Thanks" DION God Bless ya' Buddy

ZACHARY GLICKMAN
ARTISTS MANAGEMENT
19301 VENTURA BOULEVARD
SUITE 205
TARZANA, CALIFORNIA 91356-3028
(818) 708-1300

banjo, a four-string tenor banjo, a spectacular thing, with pornographic etchings on it. It was called "The Majestic," and it was beautiful. Hand-carved. I wanted to take it home. Arthur Godfrey, who was huge with his TV show *Talent Scouts*, bought it.

What is it with actors and banjos? One day Judy and I went to see the movie *King Rat*, which starred George Segal. I said to Judi, "I know I know that guy." She says, "C'mon, he's a movie actor, how do you know him?" I said, "I know him, I know him." She didn't believe me. About three days later, George Segal walks into the store. And I said, "You know, I told my wife I knew you!" He said, "Yeah, we come in every year; I bought about three banjos from you. I want another one." And he played very well. He hung out, he used to buy a lot there, sit around playing

and telling my mother stories. I used to meet him at Zabar's all the time, and we always hit it off.

We had a Gibson banjo in the window, the Gibson All-American. It was the most elaborate banjo they ever made. I kept loaning it to Charlie Osgood, who does *CBS Sunday Morning*, to play on his TV show. He

wanted to buy it. But I never wanted to sell it. I kept telling him, "Charlie, I want a *lot* of money for it." It was beautiful. It had all of American history depicted on it, from the Revolutionary War to the Civil War, World War I and II – all hand-carved. And on the back it had a very ornate American eagle on it. And Osgood really wanted it. He's quite a nice man.

Tom Chapin

"If you worked for him, you might have thought he was tough."

My dad, Jim Chapin, used to bring us into Manny's when we were little kids. Manny ran the store, and Henry was a youngster. My dad had the drum books. He wrote *Advance Techniques for Independent Coordination*. It's like a bible for drummers, and he sold them to Manny's. Dad bought me my first guitar at Manny's, my first

good one. It was an Epiphone Texan, made in Kalamazoo, Michigan, right after Gibson bought Epiphone. My daughter plays it now. I think it was $180 at the time.

I have a song I wrote about my dad, called "Distant Drummer."

I was only twelve years old when dad
  bought me my first guitar
At Manny's Music on 48th
Where they treated me like the son of a star
We never learned to play the drums,
They taught us more than just a song
And to hold the music loose in our hearts,
So we can play a whole life long.

World Hunger Year was started by my brother Harry, and every time we had a charitable event Manny's gave us a donation, and give us some instruments to raffle off. Henry was one of those guys, I imagine if you worked for him you might have thought he was tough, but he was always very generous, and his family was very supportive of us. They always treated us like superstars.

THE CHAPIN BROTHERS

HARRY CHAPIN

Manny
Warmest Regards
Dean Martin

We always had a lot of movie stars and celebrities coming in. Some of them could play, some of them couldn't.

Shirley Maclaine plays guitar very badly. Dustin Hoffman bought a Gibson Hummingbird and played it so badly it was unbelievable.

Richard Gere came in to buy an amplifier, and he wanted a Mesa Boogie. He plays well, but I said, "You know, you're a great actor, and a good guitar player, but that's a very difficult amplifier." I said the same thing to John McEnroe, who is so nice, a total gentleman, no matter what you have heard about him. I told him, "That's a very hard amplifier for an amateur to work with. You're not good enough for it. It's too precise. Buy a Peavey. Buy a Fender. I know you can afford the Mesa Boogie, but it's ridiculous. You're an amateur." My son was standing there, and he said, "How can you tell John McEnroe something like that?" I said, "Because it's the truth. If they don't want to hear it, they won't buy here." He bought the Peavey. Gere came back, too. Now

McEnroe comes in a lot. Mick Jagger brought him in one time. Vitas Gerulaitas used to come in a lot. And Guillermo Vilas. Those tennis players like to play rock 'n' roll. And also all the baseball players. The Mets. Daryl Strawberry, Keith Hernandez. All those guys, they lived in the store for a while.

Lucille Ball, and her kids came in once: Dino, Desi, and Billy, who were pop stars. Dino got killed in that horrible plane crash. I remember Lucy came in the store with him and I hardly recognized her. It was early in the morning, and she hadn't put on her face yet.

Thanks, Henry,
for the help
on the
movie scene.
I'm glad our
careers don't
depend on that
one, brother.
Yours
Kris Kristofferson

KRIS KRISTOFFERSON

NEW ADDRESS
BERTA BLOCK
Hart Block Management
888 FIFTH STREET
NEW YORK, NEW YORK
11 Bailey Avenue
Ridgefield, Conn. 06877

INTERNATIONAL FAMOUS AGENCY
A DIVISION OF MARVIN JOSEPHSON ASSOCIATES INC

I was in a film with Kris Kristofferson. They did a movie in the store, and I was on camera for about a second. He put up a picture on the wall that says: "If you don't go in to the movie business, I won't go into the music business." It's one of the first movies he ever did, and I don't know the name. But that was my movie.

We did a lot of movies in the store. Woody Allen used to shoot here, and then one day he and I had a fight. He wasn't very famous then — he wanted to borrow a soprano saxophone. I said, "No problem, I need it

"Dustin Hoffman bought a Gibson Hummingbird and played it so badly it was unbelievable."

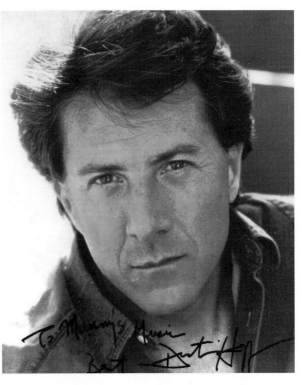

back at the end of the week." Three weeks go by, it doesn't come back. So I call him up and say, "Woody, what are you doing?" he said "Don't bug me, I can bring it back when I wanna bring it back." I said, "Woody, bring it back now or I'm gonna have to charge you." He brought it back, and he wouldn't come in to the store again. He used to send his father in every once in a while, but he wouldn't come in. And then one day Judi and I are in a restaurant and he's there. And I went over and apologized. And we made up, but he's a strange guy. A very strange guy.

We Are The Champions:
A gift from the 1986 World Series-winning New York Mets.

Pop Art: *This Strat is one of two given to Manny's by artist Peter Max.*

My absolute favorite group was the Who.

When the Who first came to New York, I got friendly with the whole group. Everyone except for Daltrey. No one could get friendly with Daltrey, because he wasn't a musician — he was a singer.

Pete Townshend would come into the store and just take a guitar off the wall and shout, "Pay you later, see ya!" If Pete saw something, he wouldn't even sign for it. He just used to take guitars: "Henry, I like this guitar. I'm gonna take it home with me. If I like it, I'll pay you for it." Toss it in the car. He did it all the time. When Townshend destroyed a piece of a equipment, it was very good for business. But it bugged me after I spent a while getting a certain instrument for him and he smashes it the first night he used it. I ask his roadie to try and stop him in time, but he never did.

Pete Townshend is a brilliant, brilliant man. He is very worldly. He's a guitar player, a good musician. There isn't a subject he isn't conversant in. He is into different kinds of music. He's creative. I really believe he'll do a great opera one of these days — if you can go by *Tommy*, which was really a folk opera.

John Entwistle came to my son's bar mitzvah, and we went to his house in England. My wife and my family, and it was just a drunken ball. His house was so big — his castle was so big, that it took us an hour to see every room. He had one room just for his bass cases. I think he bought more than anyone else because he bought horns, too. He was a horn player. And anything that came out new in trumpets or French

The kid got the guitar OK. He was knocked out naturally. The only thing is, he thought Jimmy Page had sent it! I hope they get it right in heaven.

I understand Bobby has put his dirty feet all over your nice clean floor again.

Love.

Pete Townshend

2, The Embankmet
Twickenham TW1 3DU

May 1st.

Dear Henry,

"When Townshend destroyed a piece of equipment, it was very good for business."

horns he bought. People know he that plays the French horn on some of their records, and maybe they think of it as a novelty more than anything else, but he could really play quite well. He was very talented.

Entwistle used to buy a lot of stuff at Manny's. He also liked the weird-shaped basses, like the Gibson Thunderbirds. When they stopped making them I had about fifteen left in stock. He came into the store and he

THE WHO

THE WHO

Publicity: New Action Ltd.
888 8th Ave., N.Y.C.
212-581-3257

PREMIER TALENT ASSOCIATES, INC.
200 WEST 57TH STREET
New York, N.Y. 10019 - 757-4300

bought every one of them. Gibson came out with a hollow-body bass, which I think was my idea, and he loved that. I was talking to Les Propp at Gisbon about it one day, and I said, "These guys want a hollow-body sound, but they want it electrified." And they did it. Entwistle was a great customer. He spent a lot of money, he really enjoyed his musical instruments. He could play almost anything.

We'd go out with him, and when John ordered wine, he ordered wine. He used to buy wine that was $200 a bottle. He didn't care. To him the money was nothing. This guy didn't know what money was — the Who were so poor when they were young, and then all of a sudden they were getting paid off in bags of cash. He got a check and a bag full of cash.

And they enjoyed spending it. When the movie *Tommy* came to the Ziegfield Theater, we were invited as guests of the Who to a party in the subway station at 54th Street and Sixth Avenue. When we got to the subway station it was decked out in a marvelous holiday mood. The subway station had not been opened yet. It was brand-new. There were flowers everywhere, and tables full of food. Roast beef,

The kid is alright: John Entwistle and Holly.
Above, a drawing by John and a hand-carved guitar, gifts to Manny's.

Leslie West

"I used to get my ass kissed real good..."

I worked on 47th Street in the diamond district for my uncle, and every day I walked to Manny's to price a Stratocaster. And every day it was the same price. One day on my lunch, I was 13, I stayed at Manny's for four hours and Henry tried to sell me a Guild guitar – but I had to have the Strat (although I did buy two Guild Starfires later). When I got back late to my uncle he said, "Don't come back to work ever again." So I practiced six hours a day for six years, and my uncle dropped dead because he had to deliver the diamonds instead of me.

Then I traded my Strat for a Zimgar because the Vagrants had new instruments, and I wanted a shiny new guitar. Stupid me! I used to get my ass kissed real good when I walked into Manny's. I also got inspected by Henry to see if I was on narcotics, and thirty years after the fact he still inspects me.

I think my picture should be on the front door. Just my opinion, I could be wrong.

Who Are You?
Keith Moon plants one on the Mountain man.

KEITH MOON   LESLIE WEST

shrimp, lobsters, clams, the finest Beluga caviar. There was everything you could possibly imagine. The wine and the whiskey were fantastic.

There were about 400 or 500 people at this subway party. Every celebrity under the sun was there. At the table we sat with the group, which was Pete Townshend and his wife, John and Allison Entwistle, Ann Margaret, Tina Turner, Elton John, and Keith Moon, who didn't have a chair, and sat on my lap almost all night long, calling me "Dad," and drinking an entire bottle of cognac. Keith and I were very, very close. He was one of the most gentle, beautiful young men I have ever met. When he died it was a terrible, terrible loss.

For Henry?
you and me.
We're mature!
Aren't we......?

Pete Townshend
1993

BOB DYLAN

PERSONAL MANAGEMENT: **AB**C/**M** INC./ALBERT B. GROSSMAN/JOHN COURT/75 E. 55 ST., N.Y.C.

Bob Dylan came in a few times. The guy doesn't talk to anybody, he doesn't do anything. He's different.

He bought a couple guitars from me once. Bought a flat-top Gibson. One day he was sitting looking in the window, and I went outside and I said, "Hey, Bob, what's the matter? You can't walk in the store?" He just turned around and walked away — didn't say a word. He's very introverted. I think he's just very shy. He just walks around. If he wants to buy something he tells one of his guys and they buy it. I don't think he's ever said more than five words. But he signed a photo for us. It says, "Keep one eye closed at all times."

I've known Al Kooper, who played organ with Dylan on "Like a Rolling Stone," since he was a baby. His father used to come in. In fact, the first thing he ever bought from me was a metronome. He used to drive me crazy, too. When he was with the Blues Project, he bought a lot of guitars from me. And later, with Blood, Sweat and Tears. Broke my chops

BLOOD - SWEAT + TEARS

constantly. He was a real pain in the butt sometimes, but he was a good friend, too. He still comes in and sees my kids.

Mick Jagger and David Bowie came in on Thanksgiving Eve, the Wednesday before Thanksgiving, the busiest day of the year. They spent three hours in the store. That used to be normal. Doesn't happen anymore. Nobody went near them. They do their own shtick, they had their

"I said to George, 'Leave. You're annoying me, you're annoying Mr. Montgomery.'"

own time, everybody ignored them. They just wanted to buy Christmas presents.

Keith Richards came into the store once, with his brand-new Lamborghini parked out in front — and he was pretty smashed. And the cops came in, because you're not allowed to park on 48th Street. They knew some rock star was in our store and they came in. Keith was smart enough to say, "No, it's not mine. It belongs to him." And he pointed to my son, Judd, who drove the car around the block to wait for the cops to go. They would have given Keith a much harder time.

The Doors were very good customers. Robby Krieger, the guitar player, insisted we take on Mesa Boogie, who did not want to sell to us, since we discounted, and they really did not want that. But he wanted to make sure they were available in New York. Now we do a lot of business with them.

Sly Stone always came in with his whole entourage, his band, his family. He was a lot of fun. He was wild, a very funny, happy man. He enjoyed being a superstar.

George Benson used to come into the store when he was a kid, and

Carlos Santana

"When Miles recommends something…"

I first went to Manny's not too long after the Woodstock Festival in 1969. Of course I had no way of knowing then that this was only the beginning of a long-standing relationship with Henry and this fabulous store.

Miles Davis had told me that he had a wah-wah pedal and loved it and told me that I ought to be using one. Well, when Miles recommends something. . . . My first purchase was a Crybaby pedal.

I think that all musicians gravitate to those places that sell the best instruments, so my going to Manny's should come as no surprise. The fact that I kept coming back, however, had everything to do with Henry's very attentive and knowledge-able manner. He was a "hands-on" kind of guy who treated musicians in a special manner. And the place itself was more like a museum than just another music store. All those photos of musicians I admired so much were so inspiring. And these were not just rock or jazz musicians; they came from every branch of music and to me they simply represented excellence. I remember being particularly impressed by the photos of people such as Jo Jones, Louis Armstrong, and Philly Joe Jones. Manny's was a place where you could almost feel the spirit of those musicians whose photos adorned the walls. I treasure my experiences in this wonderful place.

P. O. Box 26671
San Francisco, California 94126

You keep
Ticking me out,
and I'll keep coming
Back Henry.

Peace,
George
Benson

GEORGE BENSON

ROGERS & COWAN, INC.
3 EAST 54th STREET
NEW YORK, NEW YORK 10022

WARNER / REPRISE

he used to drive me crazy. One day he's in there taking the guitars — he wasn't famous — just taking the guitars off the racks and playing. I started to kick him out, and Wes Montgomery came in. I said to George, "Leave. You're annoying me, you're annoying Mr. Montgomery." Wes said, "Let him play, he's a pretty good player." So on the wall he has a picture: "You keep kickin' me out, and I keep comin' back."

I knew Wes very well. He had an L5 Gibson. That's all he ever wanted, but he was always looking for an amplifier sound. I got him involved with

THE BAND   Photograph by David Gahr

GROSSMAN - GLOTZER MGT.   **75 East 55th. Street**   New York, N. Y. 10022 (212) PL 2 - 8715

Bonnie Raitt

"I was excited…"

I bought my first Guild F-50 at Manny's shop in New York when I was a teenager. Manny's was legendary — I was excited to go there, I knew so many important musicians passed through. I didn't see any during my brief visits, but I remember the wonderful service and knowledge of the staff, and of course fell in love with my big F-50 Guild the moment I played it.

But I was lucky that when I started, I was able to go to the Fillmore East every weekend, see my idols, and then go to 48th Street to Manny's to further my dream. I don't believe those days will ever happen quite like that again.

BONNIE RAITT

Rolling Stones

Rolling Stones Records distributed by Atlantic Records

a company called Standel. No one had ever heard of them. When they came to New York to show the amplifier, I bought some of their stuff, and it was a good thing, because their sales manager said, "We didn't have any money to get back to California unless you bought some amps!" I think they turned out to be one of the best amplifiers ever made. And Wes heard it, and he bought it, an 82L15V. He loved the amplifier, and it was very, very popular until it was taken over by Gibson, and then it went down the drain. Gibson could never build an amplifier.

SLY AND THE
FAMILY STONE

DAEDALUS
MANAGEMENT

WILLIAM MORRIS AGENCY, INC.
EPIC RECORDS

For Henry J.
Chet Atkins C.G.P.

Chet Atkins — C.G.P.

The country music guys are great.

Willie Nelson is one of the nicest men ever. Not assuming. Used to come in with his guys. Never bought anything, but always used to hang out.

Chet Atkins, he was a very good customer. He had a friend of his named Harold Bradley, who's one of the biggest studio musicians in Nashville. He brought Chet into the store, and Chet used to buy a lot of stuff. Not guitars so much, but all sorts of synthesizers, keyboards,

To Manny's,
Thanks for being there!

photo: Timothy White

WAYLON

1117 17th Avenue South
Nashville, TN 37212
(615)329-9180

and any effect, any new effect I had, I sent out to him automatically. He didn't even ask for them. He got them, and if he didn't like it, he sent it back. If he liked it, he kept it.

When Duane Eddy first came to New York, I got him the deal with Guild Guitars, which he never gave me credit for, and for which I will never forgive him.

Duane always played Gretsch guitars, the 6120 model. And one year, the guy that owned Guild said to me, "Do me a favor, can you get Duane Eddy for me?" I said, "What are you gonna do for me?" He said, "I wanna make a guitar, a Duane Eddy model. And I'll see what I can do."

So I called him up and asked Duane, and he said, "What's in it for me?" And I said, "All the free guitars you want, maybe some cash." He said, "I'll make a deal." And he made a deal with Guild Guitars for the Duane Eddy model. He sold a lot of guitars.

To Manny's
Best to you
al way's
B.B. King +
Lucille

B.B. KING

B.B. King said that when he comes to New York, his good luck stop is Manny's.

He said this to Bo Diddley, and Bo said, "I got the same thing!" Can you imagine the two of them, sitting around just bullshitting? Bo Diddley didn't buy guitars, he had his own thing that he made, or Gretsch made. But boy, does he buy stuff. Electronics.

Sinatra used to come in once in a blue moon, but nobody could ever go near him. No one could talk to Frank unless they had permission to talk to him. He wasn't the nicest person in the world to deal with. But he sure was a talent.

The only thing Buddy Rich couldn't stand is if you were not talented. And no one, no one, played drums as well as Buddy. And that goes for Gene Krupa and Chick Webb. He was brilliant. Every drummer – every drummer that's a musician – will tell you that one year he broke his arm, and played better drums with one arm than most guys would play with four.

He liked his own way with the companies. Like if he wanted the Zildjian cymbals, you sent him a lot of Zildjians until he found the ones he liked. And then he gave the other ones away. He never sent them back.

He played Slingerland drums, but one year he got in a fight with Bud Slingerland, and he went with Ludwig. And then he went back with Slingerland, I think. He wanted everything his own way and he had the talent to get it.

The stories about him and Sinatra all were true, every one. He used to tell us that they used to have fistfights, and bloody. They never liked each other, until the end, when they became friendly. I think they respected each others' talent.

When I had my appendix out, I think I was fourteen years old, around

"The stories about Buddy Rich and Sinatra were true, every one."

1950. I was in the hospital in Far Rockaway, and Buddy came up in his brand-new Lincoln Continental convertible to the hospital. I'll never forget that car: a white Lincoln Continental, the most smashing-looking thing you ever saw. If it was new, Buddy had to have it.

Krupa was a very quiet person; I never really knew him well. But of all the big band drummers who weren't soloists, Dave Tough was the best. He played with Dorsey, he played with Goodman. He was probably the best big

Who do you love: Henry and Bo Diddley on vacation in New Orleans.

band drummer in the business. Not even Joe Morello came close. None of these guys could beat him. And if you ask any of these old-time drummers, they'll tell you how good he was.

But drummers never really bought too much gear. They had their drum set, they had their cymbals, and all they did was buy drumsticks. They never had anything to experiment with, until, of course, the electronic drums came out. And that never really made it. But drummers are an entity all to themselves. They are more ridiculed than any other musician, that's for sure.

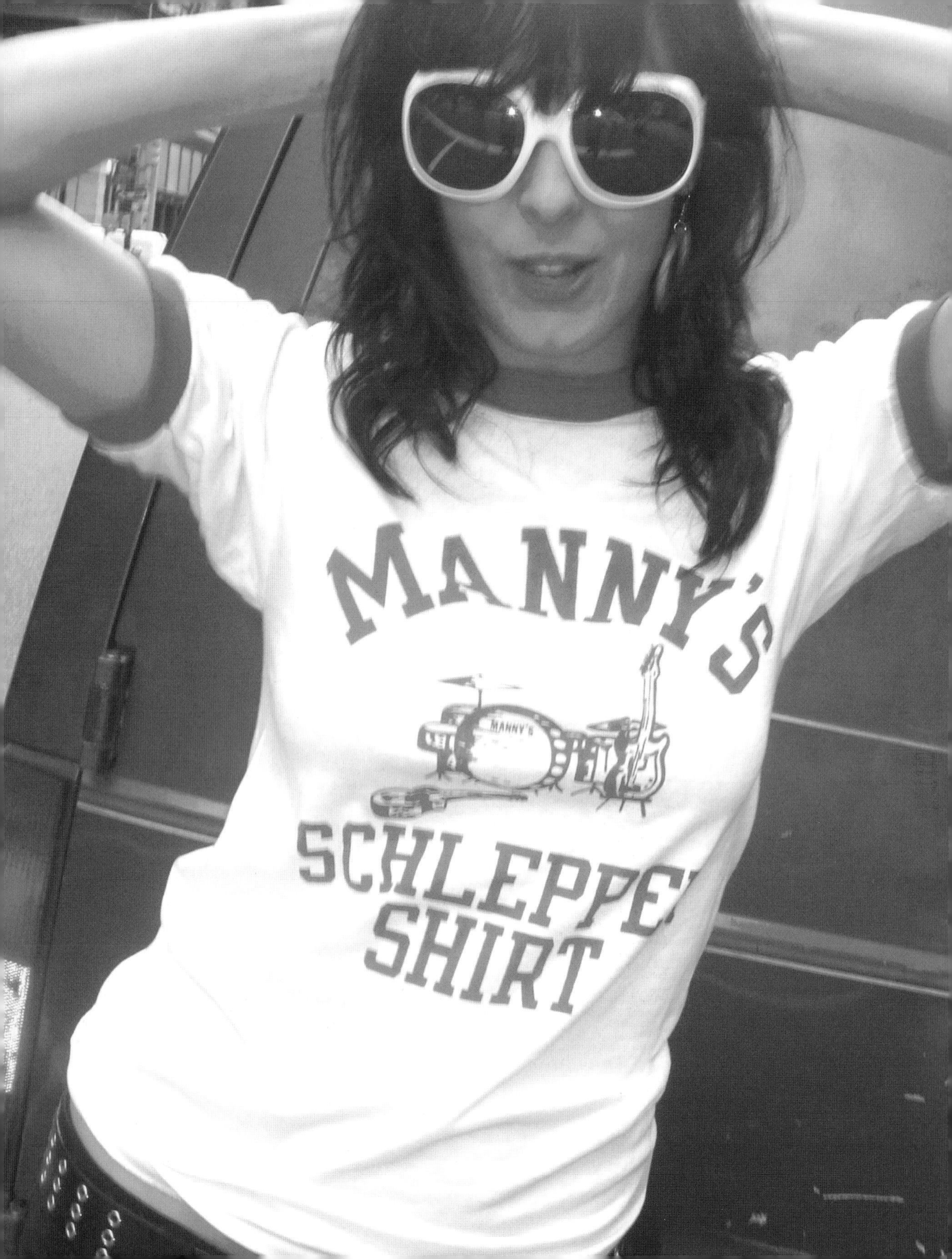
MANNY'S
MANNY'S
SHIRT

It was the Lovin' Spoonful who gave us the idea to start making shirts that said "Manny's Shleppers."

That's what they called their roadies – schleppers. We didn't sell the shirts, but every roadie got one and most of them wore them on the stage. Whether it was the Who or the Stones, one of the guys always had a Shlepper shirt on. Kids used to come and try and buy them, but we would never sell them. We wouldn't even give them to musicians for a long time, only their roadies. Eventually we gave in to the rock stars who loved them, and used to wear them on stage. At some point the business changed and musicians and roadies weren't coming in, so finally we decided to start selling them. You can still get them at Manny's.

I loved the Spoonful, I love the four of them – John Sebastian, Zal Yanovsky, Steve Boone, and Joe Butler. My mother adored Zali. He was like a bum in the street, but a loveable person. John, too, and she used to feed them both lunch. She'd give Zali and John each half of a sandwich. The "Spoonfuls" were the food my mother gave them, what they used to eat in the store. You ask Sebastian and those guys and they'll tell you, the Spoonfuls are named for lunches at Manny's.

To Manny
with my thanks
& Best wishes.
Itzhak Perlman

ITZHAK PERLMAN

Photo: Christian Steiner

IMG Artists

22 East 71st Street
New York. NY 10021

Now Itzhak Perlman, here's a man, probably the world's greatest violinist, never ever said, *Take care of me.*

And anybody that went up to him in the store, he was so gracious. One day the guitar player Vernon Reid comes in the store, and Perlman walks, in and Vernon whispers to me, "Henry, get me a picture with Itzhak Perlman?" I said, "Sure." So I said to Perlman, "The young man over there…" And he said, "You mean Vernon Reid?" Perlman is no square.

He took this electric violin once, and it had all these different effects on it, you could make any kind of sound, and within five minutes he had it down pat. And he played for us. One day he came into the store with one of his Stradivarius violins, and says, "Henry, can you do something without telling anybody? I want to try this with a pickup." I said, "You've got to be kidding me. If you scratch it, how bad are you going to feel?"

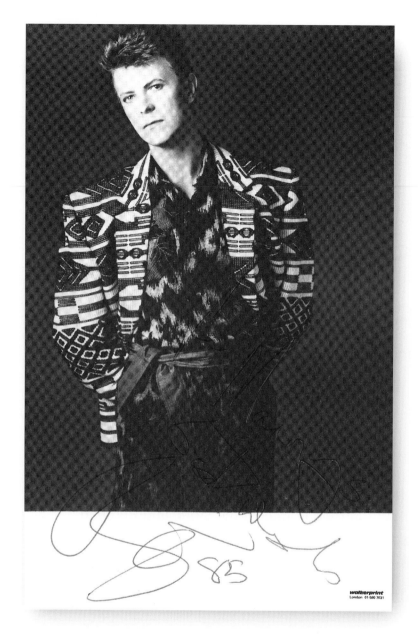

But he tried it. The man is an amazing talent. He awes me. The Beatles, Simon and Garfunkel, I've known them since they were kids, so even though they're superstars, I mean gigantic superstars, I can't be in awe of them. They're nice young kids that I've known all their lives!

Itzhak Pearlman is a man that I sit down and I can listen to him. Over all his obstacles, he's triumphed. A great, great human being. And whatever price I told him, he chiseled with me; he told me: "I'm Jewish, what do you expect!"

I've known Paul Stanley from Kiss since he was five years old, when he started playing guitar. He signed a guitar for me, "To Uncle Henry, I love you very much." He's a very nice young man. I even tried to get my daughter involved with him. He loves her and she loves him, but it never worked out. He was from Long Island, and his parents didn't have a lot

PAUL STANLEY   VINNIE VINCENT   ERIC CARR   GENE SIMMONS

RECORDS
810 SEVENTH AVENUE NYC 10019

BOOKING AGENCY: AMERICAN TALENT INTERNATIONAL
888 SEVENTH AVENUE NYC 10019

GENERAL CONTACT: GLICKMAN/MARKS MANAGEMENT
655 MADISON AVENUE NYC 10021 • (212) 752-7455

"Once in a while we had problems..."

of money. When he bought them a house, he came into my store, and said, "I just bought my parents a house out on Long Island Sound." He was so proud, he was so happy, the fact that he was able to do this for his parents. Out of all the "metallic" rock stars, he's the least metallic that I know. He's very sweet, enjoyable, not vicious, not nasty. He's got a beautiful wife now and a family. He was like my little son, my little kid.

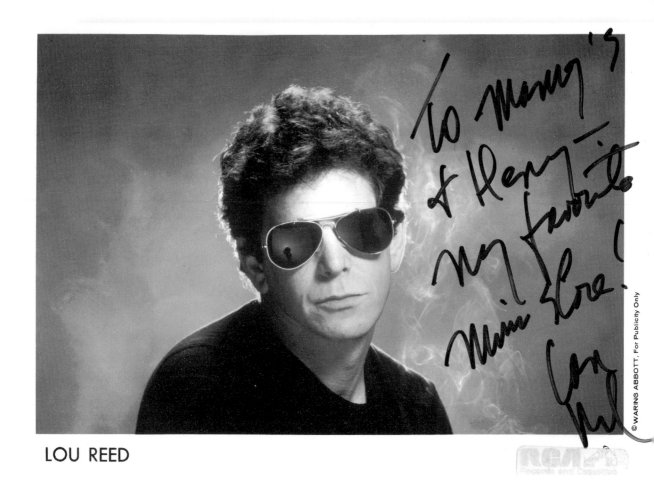

LOU REED

I truly love him.

Paul Simon is a good friend. He said in an article in *Life* magazine about how his father brought him into the store when he was seven years old to buy his first guitar. To be mentioned in *Life* magazine was a great thing. Paul Simon bought his first guitar at Manny's Music store on 48th Street in New York!

So I've known Paul since before he was with Art Garfunkel. I was like his big uncle when he started coming into the store. When he got together with Artie, I was thrilled. I have their picture on the wall from when they were still Tom and Jerry.

Lou Reed is one of the nicest guys. I like him very much. When he first got started, he was the worst druggie. I mean, he was disreputable. And he turned into one of the most intelligent young men I have ever met. I have him on the wall – his first entry, when he was a druggie. Skinny and horrible. Today he's healthy. He took up golf.

I get along with him very well. When Lou was on drugs, I let him charge stuff. And he owed me about a thousand dollars for a couple of years. He never forgot me for that. Now he spends a few thousand every month, and he always pays his bills. Now he argues with Dino DiMucci

"Lou Reed is one of the nicest guys. I like him very much."

about who has their picture on the wall more.

Carole King was so nice. She would kiss me every time they came in. I had a problem with a customer, who was angry for some reason. Carole was in the store and she said, "Hey, these guys are great, they would never cheat you or anything." And they walked out very happy.

Once in a while we had problems. One day a kid came in the store, picked out an amplifier, and said to the guy standing next to him, "How much is this amp?" The guy told him $200, just pay me, and I'll write it up for you up front. Of course the guy didn't work here. He took the money and walked out the door. The kid's mother comes in and starts screaming. I said, "Listen, I didn't tell him to give the guy the money. He's a stupid kid." So she called me for calling him stupid as well as the two hundred dollars. So we went to the small claims court, and the case was thrown out, of course, but the judge asked me to apologize to her son for calling him a moron.

In the late 1930s, Manny decided that musicians' pictures on the walls would save money on painting – and all the musicians thought it would be cool to be on the wall. That's how the world famous collection began. It was that simple…

L - R : MALCOLM YOUNG, BRIAN JOHNSON, ANGUS YOUNG, PHIL RUDD, CLIFF WILLIAMS

PHOTO CREDIT : MICHAEL HALSBAND

eastwest records america / EEG

We can't forget MR STILL

To Mummy! Magic Steven Tyler

AEROSMITH

Thanks to Henry, Rick, Bill, and all the guys at Mummy's 3/26/86 Tom Hamilton

Photo / Ron Pownall

Columbia
7912

Ian Anderson

Hello Henry
Hello Stuart
and love and hate to all at Mummy's

Jethro Tull

Chrysalis
Please Credit Brian Ward Mar. 1976

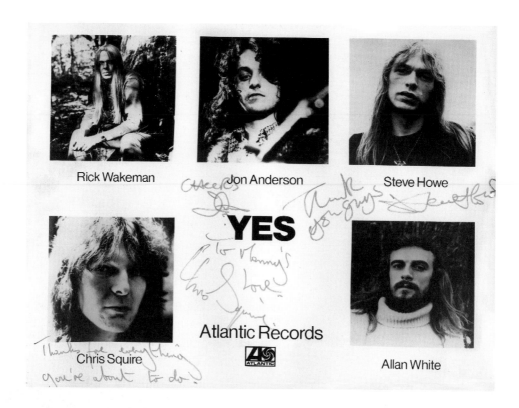

Rick Wakeman   Jon Anderson   Steve Howe

YES

Chris Squire   Atlantic Records   Allan White

Ian McDonald • Mick Jones • Lou Gramm • Al Greenwood • Ed Gagliardi • Dennis Elliott

FOREIGNER

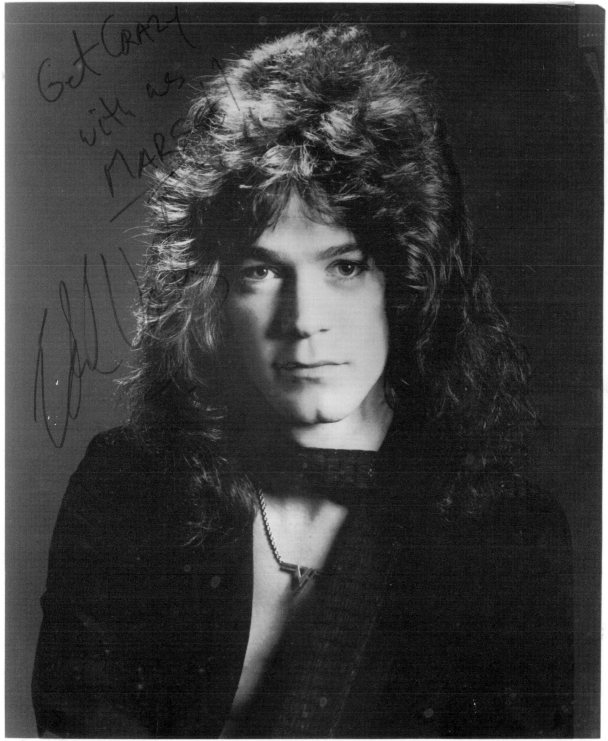

 EDWARD VAN HALEN

New York Dolls

Recording Exclusively For

A product of Phonogram, Inc.

RAMONES

Photo by: George DuBose

Blondie

Chrysalis

THE CARS

To Mannis,

Thanks for all your help
over all these years.
We don't 4get. Rockon......

With Love,,
Joan
Jett

Joan Jett and the Blackhearts

FLEETWOOD MAC

THE ALLMAN BROTHERS BAND   CAPRICORN RECORDS   PHIL WALDEN & ASSOCIATES, INC.

New Riders Of The Purple Sage

To
Henry
and all the boys
at Manny's
The musicians Disneyland!
All the Best!
Al DiMeola

AL
DiMEOLA

Henry Weston Rell
for your
knowing
kind one

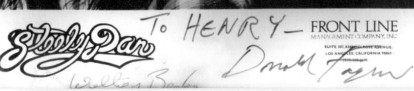
To HENRY —

Steely Dan

Walter Becker

FRONT LINE
MANAGEMENT COMPANY, INC.

SUITE 307, 8380 MELROSE AVENUE,
LOS ANGELES, CALIFORNIA 90069 ·
(213) 655-4600

Donald Fagen

abc Records

Stanley Clarke

Lenny White   To Henry   Bill Connors

Chick Corea

RETURN TO FOREVER FEATURING CHICK COREA

CAPTAIN BEEFHEART

Exclusive Representation:
Regular Moon Management
281 Bartlett Street
San Francisco, CA 94110
(415) 821-1212

Twiggy Ramirez   Zim Zum   Marilyn Manson   Ginger Fish   Madonna Wayne Gacy

MARILYN MANSON

nothing

J. J. French

"Kid, you better be good, or have money, or get out!"

Sometime around 1965, my older brother Jeff took me into Manny's, where he had bought a guitar in 1958. It was a Guild acoustic. It was eighty-five dollars. My brother paid Henry five dollars a week until it was paid off. Henry always remembered my brother's name, and even the serial number of the guitar. My brother introduced me to Henry in 1965.

I bought my second electric guitar from Henry in 1968; it was a Gibson SG Special. It cost $242.50. I also bought a Fender P-Bass (black with maple neck) in 1970 for $200. I bought an Ampeg V-4 stack for $600 in 1969, and my first Marshall stack in 1970 for $900. If you had rock 'n' roll dreams like mine, walking into Manny's was like entering the gates of heaven.

I used to go at least once a week for years. My dad worked in the jewelry district around the corner. When the store was in its original location down the street, I saw a Gibson gold-top Les Paul in the window. This was in January 1968. I fell in love with this model and I have collected goldtops ever since that day.

During the period of 1964–1970, I don't think there existed a Mecca of dreams like Manny's anywhere else in the world. You always had the feeling that you would meet a rock star in Manny's. It was the gold standard, and you almost didn't feel worthy of being there. It was dripping with the New York attitude. It was almost like there was a sign at the door that said, "Kid, you better be good, or have money, or get out!" It was as New York as you could get, in a "Damon

Twisted Sister

Runyon way," with characters like Henry, Stu, and Bill running around with that yellow guitar that became a symbol of the store.

My band, Twisted Sister, became popular on Long Island in the '70s. We sold 10 million albums, 35 gold and platinum records worldwide, and played 9,000 shows over 30 years, and I didn't get to go to Manny's as much as I used to.

But I was lucky that when I started, I was able to go to the Fillmore East every weekend, see my idols, and then go to 48th Street to Manny's to further my dream. I don't believe those days will ever happen quite like that again.

MADHOUSE
MANAGEMENT

TED NUGENT

ATLANTIC

THE TURTLES

CARLY SIMON

To All our friends at Manny's,

To Henry & To

people have the power

PATTI SMITH

Photo: Annie Leibovitz

ARISTA

THE VELVET UNDERGROUND   **EXCLUSIVELY ON MGM/ VERVE RECORDS**

R-1711

THE PRETENDERS
MALCOLM FOSTER, CHRISSIE HYNDE, MARTIN CHAMBERS, ROBBIE McINTOSH

Management
James Cotton Mgmt.
Thomas Heimdal
PH. (312) 943-8426
FAX (312) 943-7879

Booking
Day & Night Productions
Patrick Day
PH. (410) 521-6416
FAX (410) 521-6420

JAMES COTTON

PHOTO CREDIT : CAROL FRIEDMAN

To Manny's
Best,
Warren Zevon

WARREN ZEVON

reprise

Photo Credit: Diego Uchitel

For Heavy &
All the folks at Manny's
from Steve Reich 1/91

photo: Deborah Feingold

STEVE REICH

Best Wishe, Manny's

Photo CHRIS CALLIS

PHILIP GLASS

IPA IPA INTERNATIONAL PRODUCTION ASSOCIATES, INC.
853 BROADWAY   ROOM 2120   NEW YORK CITY 10003
TEL. 212.505.1688   TELEX: 821238

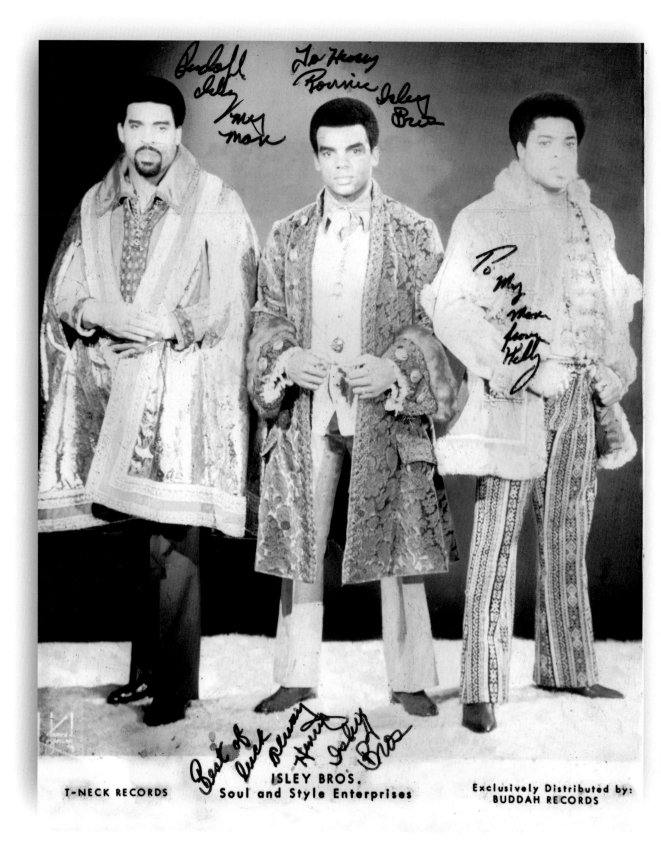

ISLEY BRO'S.
Soul and Style Enterprises

T-NECK RECORDS

Exclusively Distributed by:
BUDDAH RECORDS

To Manny's
You are The Greatest!

Gene Redd

Yuri

"KOOL & THE GANG"   Personal Mgt.   9/11/71

Bob

Henk

Butch

SALT
PEPPER
and

MNEMONICS

area Code Code
JANET 757-9766   203

To My old friend)
Manny — the
best of the best —
Thanks for
everything,
Gregg Allman
1992'

GREGG ALLMAN

To Henry,
Stuart and
all the
lads at
"Manny's"

Peter Frampton (signature)

Peter Frampton

A&M
RECORDS

Printed in U.S.A.

Herbie Hancock

DR. JOHN

ATCO

WILLIAM MORRIS AGENCY. INC

NEW YORK
BEVERLY HILLS
CHICAGO
LONDON
ROME
PARIS
MADRID
MUNICH

MALCOLM YOUNG   BRIAN JOHNSON   CHRIS SLADE   ANGUS YOUNG   CLIFF WILLIAMS

AC/DC   ATCO

IRON MAIDEN   EMI

To Stewart
Henry &
All at
Manny's

BILLY IDOL   Direction/Management: LUCOIN
                                    MANAGEMENT INC

Chrysalis

TO HENRY AND S,
LOTS OF LUCK

Distributed by CBS RECOR

BOB MARLEY Manny is the beat
Bob Marley.
ISLAND

Paul Schaffer

"It was like getting an *alea*."

George Benson, Henry, and Paul Schaffer at the Jimmy Maelen Memorial Golf Tournament.

When I first moved to New York it was to play the piano in the pit for *The Magic Show*, which was a popular Broadway play. The show played at the Cort theatre on 48th Street, right besides Manny's. For a year, I went to work every day there, and I'd often go in to Manny's just to look at the pictures on the wall. I was especially impressed by the British rock groups, with inscriptions made out to Henry. It was history. I bought my first synthesizer at Manny's, an Oberheim OBX-A, which I used on the record "He's So Shy" with the Pointer Sisters in 1980.

I got to know Henry when he took an interest in a memorial golf tournament that some of my friends were organizing in memory of our friend, the great percussionist Jimmy Maelen. Jimmy died of leukemia. I think he was the greatest percussionist on the studio scene in the '70s and early '80s. He could play any style — Latin, rock, pop — and knew exactly what to play. He was also a sweetheart of a guy, and Henry helped with that tournament. It was a lovely thing for Henry to do.

Jimmy was a golfer and it was appropriate. And it gave me an idea of the size of Henry's heart — it was huge. He was a very sentimental guy, who I could see had helped out musicians all through the years.

Everybody went to Manny's. It was like getting an *alea* – that's when in synagogue, you're called to read the Torah. Manny's was where I met Chuck Jackson, the great rhythm and blues singer. I remember there was a guy, a street musician in the '70s, a little off mentally, who would bend over and play drumsticks on the pavement. We'd see him every day when we went from studio to studio to do jingle dates. He would be bent over, playing the sticks on the street. I remember him buying a brand new pair of sticks at Manny's, paying the cashier, and them taking the plastic wrap off and going outside to bend over and play the pavement. When you needed anything musical, you went to Manny's. It was as natural as getting an *alea* on Saturday morning.

Henry's generosity and love for the New York musician could never have been better exemplified than his support for the Jimmy Maelen Memorial Golf Outing. Even though the costs increased year after year, Henry never flinched. He just dug a little deeper, and the music vendors, manufacturers and related companies rallied with their support and generous donations. It was so gratifying to see their response just by mentioning Henry Goldrich's name. Henry saved the day a number of times.

–Jack Cavari

I never saw Henry come out from behind the counter, except for once, when he took me in the back to show me an X-rated, hand-tooled leather guitar strap someone had made. I bought it on the spot and still use it — that was thirty-five years ago!

–Will Lee

173

To Manny's —
Relax!
Love,
Billy

BILLY JOEL

8506

Billy Joel needed an Italian-style accordion, and we found it for him. He was very happy to get it.

He bought electronic pianos. He got a Fender Rhodes from us.

The Rhodes was a very popular thing. The Rhodes wasn't really portable; it weighed a ton. But it was the first piano that was moveable. And it had the piano touch. That's what the musicians all wanted. They had all these organs, and the feel of the organ was completely different than the feel of a piano, striking the hammers. And a lot of the companies tried to come out with organs that had piano sensitivity, and they just couldn't do it. Fender was the only one. Then they came along with this piano bass, which sounded like a bass fiddle or an electric bass, but it was a piano keyboard. I think the guy in the Doors used one.

Harold Rhodes was the inventor of the Rhodes piano. He's a very interesting man. He was on his own, and then he went to work, not for Fender, but with Fender. They kind of pushed him, because they had the money. I really liked Harold; he was a great man.

Speaking of keyboards, Yamaha changed everything in 1983 when

The greats get the greatest sounds on Fender-Rhodes

A new and exciting experience awaits the pianist who performs upon the 6 octave 73 key Fender-Rhodes piano. An improved and more powerful amplifier, actually two in one, boasts a 200 watt peak performance. Each of two independent power modules supplies four heavy duty speakers for maximum output. The vibrato switch, when turned on, assures a constant flow of power and presents a stereo sound never before obtainable. Suitable for any bandstand, this beautiful electric portable suitcase piano comes complete with four speakers, amplifier stand and sustaining pedal. The cabinets are constructed of strong wood and covered with durable black Tolex vinyl. A fiberglass cover is easily removed for access to harp assembly and action.

FREE 1969 CATALOG / Write Fender Musical Instruments, Dept. DB-10, 1300 East Valencia, Fullerton, Calif. 92631.

CBS Musical Instruments Columbia Broadcasting System, Inc.

Joe Zawinul with Cannonball Adderly

~ Ramsey Lewis

they came out with the DX7. It was the first affordable digital, program-mable synthesizer. That was an amazing, amazing device, one of the biggest changes in the business. Every keyboard player wanted one. And Yamaha wouldn't sell it me because I didn't have the proper place to display it! They sold it to Sam Ash, my biggest competitor, who have their shop right next door. But a lot of people who shopped at Manny's wouldn't go to Ash. So we bootlegged them, which means we bought them from other dealers. So we had them anyway, and since I was sell-ing them to professionals, Yamaha decided it was ridiculous to do busi-ness this way, especially since no one could say "I bought my DX7 at Manny's." It wasn't kosher. So they gave us the line.

"Zappa said to me, 'Henry, you know what you gotta do? You gotta open a store in Russia.'"

Stevie Wonder came in the store one day, and we had a brand-new type of synthesizer in, no one knew how to work it. But he is a genius. I mean, whatever he touches, it is amazing. So he comes in, and we have this synthesizer, no one ever saw anything like it in their lives. He tried it out, he flips, and they put it in a car and he takes it home with him. He gets it home and we get a phone call from him. I said "Stevie, what's the matter?" He said, "The instructions are not in the box." I told him, "Stevie, the instructions have to be in the box, it's a brand-new box!" He said, "What do you think I am? Blind?" He really made the synthesizer popular. He knew exactly what he was doing.

Of all of the different companies that were making synthesizers at the time, Moog was still the best. When the Minimoog first came out in 1971, Bob Moog came in to us. I didn't know anything about synthesizers. He taught me one thing: how to make it sound like a bomb coming down.

Stevie Wonder · InnerVisions

And I had a couple of salesmen who were marvelous with electronics. We used to play with that, and we really sold a lot of Moog synthesizers. That, the ARP, and Alan Perlman — a few synthesizer companies really changed things.

Moog also made a theremin. One day, Frank Zappa came in the store. Frank and I were very friendly. He was probably the most brilliant man I ever met in my whole life. Whatever you wanted to talk about, he knew, and knew well. And he tries this thing out, and he bought ten of 'em. Ten theremins. I don't know what he was going to use them for. The Moog theremin. He loved it.

 PRESS: TOTEM POLE (213) 654-1473
8255 Sunset Boulevard, Hollywood, California 90046

ELTON JOHN

MCA RECORDS

MANNY from The MOTHERS
= IT CAN'T HAPPEN HERE"

BUNK   DON   FRANK

JIM

JIM   BILLY   ROY

Zappa said to me, "Henry, you know what you gotta do? You gotta open a store in Russia." I said, "You gotta be crazy!" He said, "I'm going to Russia tonight or tomorrow night; I want you to come with me and we'll open up a store there together." I said, "Whaddaymean? How'm I gonna do that? I have no passport, I have no visa." "Don't worry, I'll take care of everything. You don't need a passport; you don't need a visa. We're gonna go to Russia and open up a store." I didn't go to Russia, no. But he was serious.

Rolling Stone

Manny's: music store of the stars

By ROB FLEDER

THE PICTURES TELL THE story. They cover the walls of Manny's Musical Instruments—hundreds of photographs, making up a veritable who's who in the history of popular music. They're all there: the Dixieland bands of the Thirties, the frontmen for the big bands of the Forties, the early rockers, the bluesmen, the folkies and, most prominently, the rogues'

crazy, until Wes Montgomery came in one day while Benson was trying a guitar and said, 'Whoa, this kid *plays*.' After that, George was allowed to hang out here."

Such aspiring and established professionals now account for ninety-five percent of Manny's trade. If asked what keeps Manny's reputation alive among the pros, Goldrich will mention the store's service, its prices, its highly qualified sales staff (most of whom are

Simon has been a constant customer since the days when he and Garfunkel were known as Tom and

Henry Goldrich - Manny's

by Martin Porter

What do

Peter Townshend, Eric Clapton, Charlie Parker, Phil Ramone, The Beatles, George Benson, Rick Derringer and Other Musicians

Have in Common?

48th STREE

Guitar Worl

They used to throw the guy out of Manny's. The salesmen were getting sick and tired of this young black guy who would come in, pick himself off the rack, and sit down play for hours on end. He didn't He just played.

the salesmen were used to the There were hundreds of them on Street, in New York—the kids dreams and a touch, maybe

enough. Just before he threw the kid out, Wes Montgomery happened into the store and caught some stray licks coming from the guitar corner of the room. Montgomery struck up a conversation with the guitarist and told Henry on the way out the door that the kid had something special.

Henry Goldrich never threw George Benson out of his store again.

There are hundreds of stories like this on 48th Street— it's a street which offers a chronicle of the New

It was there that Charlie P and his bebop gang used to ja an upstairs loft, where Phil Ra cut his engineering and produ teeth at the original A&R Reco where a bar called Jim and A served as a clearinghouse and wa hole for every musician who through New York, where Fred A had his first dancing school, and Sammy Davis was once spotted ing a fierce battle with Ray E in the middle of the street.

« GQ august » « objects of desire »

oldrich told aul Simon at "Simon nd Garfunkel" as a lousy name. He

MANNY'S HAPPY RETURNS

New York City's West 48th Street

Where Music Walks With History

'm a born and bred New Yorker, and I have been doing business on West 48th Street since I began play-

opening on West 48th Street by 1936, '37. By 1945 there were 25 to 30 stores on the block. After the war there were about 15 stores left on the street. In 1969, Rockefeller

PILOT PROGRAM UNITES RETAILERS & MUSIC THERAPISTS

MUSIC INC.

November 1994 $3

BETTER
Phone-in Drum Clinic
7 Customer-Se
Building a Wel
Compensation

Old Store, New Tricks

Tradition Meets Ambition at Manny's Music

Page 36

Inside Manny's Drum Shop

First Jobs & What They Taught

Drum Shoppers Tell All

The way it used to be is that the guys who ran the music companies were all music guys. They knew music.

They knew the business. Jerry Ash, who is the son of Sam Ash, was my biggest competitor, and had to be one of my best friends, which is quite amazing in the music business. In any business. We used to go every year, with our wives, all together, to the Frankfurt Fair, a music industry event. And as we got on the airplane, all the instrument companies would get very upset. They used to say to us all the time, "You guys can't go on the same plane!" because God forbid our plane crashed – they'd have a big problem. In the business, we were mortal enemies, but outside the business, we were the best of friends. That's what was so good about our business years ago. It was a handshake business. You gave your word to something, that was it.

I remember one night at the Frankfurt Fair, after the show was over, all of the dealers went downstairs to the bar. We all drank a lot. Nobody ever took drugs, we didn't even know what a drug looked like, but alcohol was very big. We used to go to the bar, and I bought you a drink, you bought

Jerry Ash

"We got clobbered."

Ever since I can remember, the words "48th Street" struck fear in my heart. 48th Street was lined with music shops both at ground level and in lofts one flight up. The dominant store was Manny's Music, which was the proverbial 800-pound gorilla.

Every important musician of the swing era and later of the rock era went to Manny's. Naturally all the Brooklyn kids wanted to rub elbows with the stars. A three-cent ride got them to New York from anywhere in Brooklyn. This of course made Manny's a great source of frustration for our family.

I joined the family music business in 1946, and my brother Paul and I gradually made some progress. By the middle 1960s we had three stores.

At that time, Al Wolfe, who owned Frank Wolfe Drummer's Supply directly next to Manny's, was looking to retire. Having lived in Manny's shadow for his entire career, he hated and envied them, and was looking for revenge. He sold his store to us solely because he thought we could do the most damage to them.

Coming to 48th Street was a revelation. Manny's was a far tougher competitor than we ever imagined. They had far more stock that we had, in a store twice the size of ours. Not only that, since they were doing more business in one store than we were doing in four, they could insist on first deliveries of hot new products. We got clobbered our first few years on the block.

Between the Manny's mystique and their huge stock, we could only get the leftovers. But something good did come out of this. I met Henry Goldrich, Manny's son, and his wife Judi. They are two of the sweetest people I have ever known. Our backgrounds were similar.

We managed to be close friends as well as bitter rivals. We went all over the world together, and never discussed business. One small triumph for our side: at Judi's fortieth birthday party I went over to inspect the band. I noticed that the head on the drummer's snare drum was stamped Sam Ash Music!

Jerry Ash: The cat that swallowed the 800-pound gorilla.

me a drink, it was very friendly. Bud Slingerland and Armand Zildjian were drinking, and Bud said to Armand, "You're not as big as me, I could take you any time." Right in the middle of the bar they started wrestling, just kidding, but to see two men in their fifties, icons in the music business, wrestling? We laughed for days. That's the way it was in the old days. Boy, it sure has changed.

"Icons in the music business, wrestling? We laughed for days. That's the way it was in the old days. Boy, it sure has changed."

When I started at Manny's after my stint in the Army in the '50s, we were still selling mostly to big bands and orchestras. We had a very good horn business. The biggest-selling single item was the saxophone. We used to sell clarinets and trumpets by the dozen. It was nothing to sell four, five tenor saxophones, four or five altos, a couple of trumpets — in a day. Today if you sell one a week, it's amazing.

That's how we got started, that's how my father got started. And that stuck until the '60s. Elvis really made rock 'n' roll what it is, and then the Beatles launched the guitar business. When they started playing on television, with these different instruments, wow. Like the Rickenbacker, that little black one that Lennon played? We used to sell one a year, and then we went to one a day. I mean, guitars skyrocketed, and it was all because of rock 'n' roll and especially the Beatles.

In the '60s and the '70s, there was a lot of new, different things. Sound effects, all the fuzz-tones, and the wah-wah pedals, and the '80s synthesizers. There was a lot of innovation. All through those years the music business blossomed. It went from a mom and pop-type business to millions and millions of dollars a year.

Bill Schultz

"Payday was like going to the bank."

Henry was the icon of the business back in the day, and he's the icon of good memories today. I first called on Henry when I was with Yamaha. Henry was the kind of guy who always had time for you. He'd write up the order, and he'd be racing up and down the counter. But you'd get your order, and then you'd have to go to dinner with him. He always had something nice to say about your company, but sometimes he also had something nasty, too, and then you'd have to listen to him and make a change. He knew everybody in the business. And if he knew some of the top artists or their head roadies would be there, he'd keep them around so you could make that connection. They came from all over the world to Manny's on 48th Street.

In the early days, we had these relationships with independent dealers, you knew their kids, you went to lunch, you shared problems and misery, and then it started with the big "box" stores. But an independent is a destination. You go there for strings, and lessons. You go there for knowledge, and this is what we encouraged our independents to enforce. They have to keep their people trained.

At least these big stores can get a guitar into a kid's hands. There are millions of people who go into these stores who never go into a music store. And then maybe you can get him to take lessons, and buy their second guitar. But I wouldn't build the future of the business with them. They have too many terms. It's no fun. It's got to be people, from the vendor, to the dealer, to the customer, right down the line. Musicians are begging to come into the Fender custom shop, and then they

spend all day there! You've got to be careful — they stop people from working!

No matter who it is, people touch music. There is a passion there that you must preserve. Mass marketers don't care how well a kid does on his instrument. They just want the thing out of their store. And that's what our independents will never let out of their grasp.

When I went to Fender in the '80s, Henry had already been one of the biggest Fender dealers. Fender was having its problem with quality then; at the end of the CBS years it got away from them. But I promised him that this was going to come to and end, and I asked for his support, and he gave it. Totally.

When we came into Fender, I brought all musicians with me. Maybe they didn't now how to do balance sheets, but they knew how to play the guitar, how to build it, and how to repair it. We had a strong code of quality. Each person was responsible for their work. Nothing passes out of our factory unless it is one hundred percent.

With the Internet, there is good news and no bad news. The good news is that all of your models are exposed to everyone. But when there's no tax, or huge discounts, it affects the local dealers. But you've got to learn to compete with this. It's tough as hell. But Henry was a good friend to the business You could trust him. Payday was like going to the bank. He was always there.

Bill Schultz was the CEO of Fender Musical Instruments from 1985 to 2005.

When the Isley Brothers came into the store, I think it was 1959 — it was one of our first giant sales — they came in with a paper bag filled with cash. Of course they obviously had people behind them who weren't too savory. But rock 'n' roll has changed. Now you can have a band in your bedroom — you don't even need a band — and become a star. In the 1990s we lost out on a lot business. Now you can get on a computer, buy something, if you don't like it, send it back. It's on a credit card, so you don't worry about it. And that really hurts business.

And musicians have changed so much. For instance, the horn players today are not like the older cats, who used to change mouthpieces all the time. Doc Cheatham, who was a very famous trumpet player, went on a mouthpiece kick one year — couldn't get the right mouthpiece. And I think he came in every day for at least three weeks, four weeks, buying different mouthpieces, and returning the next day and trying another one, trying another one. That was what the old musicians did. They never just picked up a saxophone like they do today and said, "Oh, that's good." Clarinetists were the worst. A clarinet player had to have a certain timbre; they went through clarinets. If you had a good player in, you had to put out eight, ten clarinets for them to pick one. Years ago, when wanted to buy a good guitar, if you want to buy a good Martin, for example, they used to go through eight guitars just to find one that suited them. Today I don't think that most of the musicians today have the desire, or the love of the instrument. I think it's more love of the money

they're gonna make out of it. The kids today, they're all electronic experts. Everything is done digitally.

That's the Internet. And you can't knock it. And as far as buying gear, they sell you what you ask for, but the idea of having the explanation, the touch, of a professional helping you out, is very important.

To work at Manny's, you have to know your instrument, you have to know the business, you have to know what you are selling. You have to take care of your customers. You have to know who your customers are. We had these people working for us — if they sold guitars, they played guitar. If they sold horns, they played horns. They had to have a personality, they couldn't walk around grumpy. They couldn't walk around with a scowl on their face. They had to be able to talk to people, to get along with people, to be prompt and honest. Well, I think everyone of them stole a little bit from me here and there. The thing we sold the most of, without a doubt is drum sticks. We sold them by the hundreds of thousands, but I never sold a pair of sticks to anyone that ever worked in the drum department. Come to think of it, I never sold a single guitar string to any of the guys who worked for me that played guitar...

About the Authors

Henry Goldrich was the proprietor of Manny's Music until 1999. He has been married to wife Judi for forty-eight years. They have three children and are proud grandparents to seven grandchildren. Henry lives in New Jersey and Florida.

Holly Goldrich Schoenfeld is Henry Goldrich's only daughter. She is a married mother of two children and lives in New Jersey. She is honored to be a part of this project.